IMAGES
of America

MARENGO
THE FIRST 100 YEARS

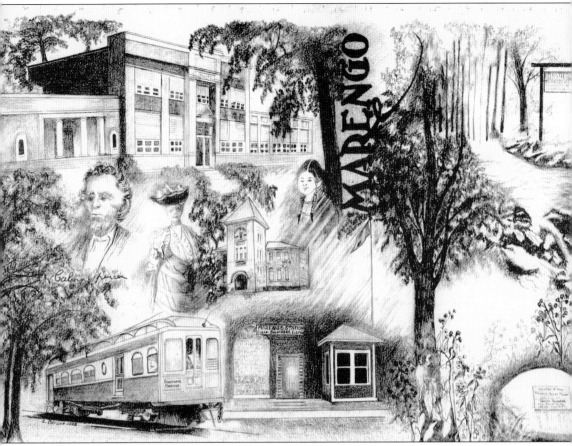

Interspersed among the majestic elm trees that lined Marengo streets, artist Lillian Higgins Bright drew this postcard in honor of Marengo's sesquicentennial in 1985. Portrayed are Calvin Spencer; Princess Kishwaukee, daughter of Chief Big Thunder; Elgin-Belvidere Electric Railroad and station; Maude Lundgren, wife of Carl Lundgren, Cubs pitcher; the Marengo Public Library; the Marengo Community High School; the grade school; the Kishwaukee River, and Indian Oaks and Calvin Spencer Parks. (Courtesy of Lillian Higgins Bright.)

On the cover: In this early-1940s photograph, the lovely old storefronts still exist; false storefront facades were at least 30 years in the distance. The vitality of the central business district is evident by the number of cars. No semi trucks are visible as the railroads still carried the majority of raw and finished supplies to the communities. It was a good time in the history of Marengo. (Courtesy of Jeanette Mack Marks.)

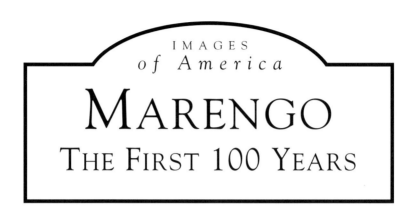

IMAGES
of America

MARENGO
THE FIRST 100 YEARS

Marengo Society for Historic Preservation

ARCADIA
PUBLISHING

Published by Arcadia Publishing
Charleston SC, Chicago IL, Portsmouth NH, San Francisco CA

Printed in the United States of America

Library of Congress Catalog Card Number: 2007930505

For all general information contact Arcadia Publishing at:
Telephone 843-853-2070
Fax 843-853-0044
E-mail sales@arcadiapublishing.com
For customer service and orders:
Toll-Free 1-888-313-2665

Visit us on the Internet at www.arcadiapublishing.com

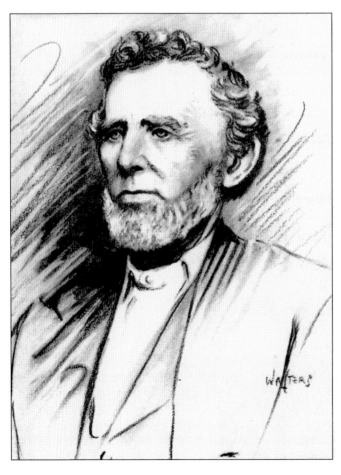

"Calvin Spencer arrived in Marengo in the company of his brother-in-law and his family. They at once built a small log house and Mr. Spencer returned to Indiana for his wife and three children. His father and mother, Mr. and Mrs. Moses Spencer, also returned with Calvin. For sixty-four years Mr. Spencer lived here, seeing the country pass from its then wild state into a densely populated country with cultivated farms and thriving villages and cities. On April 17, 1898, Calvin Spencer departed this life in fullness of years and of works well done. Years of patient toil and discouragements, all these were endured with patience and a faith in the future, until its hopes and expectations were realized." This quote is from Helen Spencer Anthony, 1935.

CONTENTS

ACKNOWLEDGMENTS

Although Marengo has only had an official historical society since 2002, there have been notable love affairs between our local residents and their Marengo history for many years. The Marengo Society for Historic Preservation, as editors of this book, owe our most heartfelt appreciation to those individuals.

Rising to the top of the list is Rudy Husfeldt. Rudy graduated from Marengo Community High School in 1927 and became a printer by trade. It was the *Beacon News* newspaper that provided the forum for Rudy, in his "retirement" years, to share his true love. Under the questionable lineage of Bossy the cow and Pete the raven, Rudy shared the facts relating to Marengo history. Then in 1969, two young local residents, Barbara McGovern and Mike Bigalke were married. Many wonder if they spent their honeymoon looking for objects relating to Marengo history! These two resources have provided the basis of Marengo's early history.

Josephine Oakley started collecting Marengo artifacts as a fairly young woman. She and Alice Wagner, historian for the Marengo Public Library, have generously shared their significant resources with the society.

In 1985, Alderman Dorothy Otis, Doria Kelley, and many others, responded to a request from the City of Marengo to provide something special for Marengo's sesquicentennial celebration. The result was the publication of *Ruminations, Reflections and Expectations.* In the early 1990s, Oakley and the Bigalkes, along with dedicated committee members, spearheaded the publication of two unbelievably valuable books relating to the history of homes on Grant Highway, Washington Street, and Prairie Street. Last, but definitely not least, are those early settler families who left us with first-person accounts of settling in the Marengo community. Martha Crissey Buell's family photo album and Frank J. Mack's 1940–1950 community photographs have been a much appreciated resource. The society's great appreciation for its "big sister," the McHenry County Historical Society as well as Cindy Miller Design, goes without saying. To these folks and the many individuals who entrusted us with their mementoes and pictures, the society expresses their sincerest appreciation!

INTRODUCTION

As early settlers moved westward into northern Illinois, they encountered landscapes, soil conditions, and native vegetation that varied from place to place. As one might expect, these settlers were looking for conditions that would provide them with an immediate and adequate supply of fresh water, wild game, and timber for building and firewood. They also wanted fertile soil to sustain their future crops. According to the records of McHenry County, these conditions were found in two 1835 principle settlements: the Virginia Settlement in the eastern part of the present township of Dorr and the Pleasant Grove Settlement, now known as the Marengo community. A visitor to Marengo in October 1855 described Marengo as follows:

> The village of Marengo, McHenry County, Illinois, is situated in the south-east corner of the township bearing the same name. The Chicago & Galena Union Railroad passes through the northern part of the village, while Pleasant Grove, the largest and noblest of the many groves which adorn and enrich our county, skirts its southern confine. Kishwaukee Prairie lies unfolded in all its loveliness at its very feet, making a panorama of woodland, village and prairie unsurpassed in northern Illinois for beauty. Nature has indeed been lavish with her gifts here and the early settlers who cast their lots upon the banks of the Kishwaukee have ever boasted of possessing the Garden of the County.

How did nature create such a beautiful setting? During the Ice Age, advancing continental glaciers bulldozed and reshaped the landforms of the upper Midwest. As the massive glaciers slowly melted away and deposited their loads of soil and rock, the Marengo area was left with a large glacial moraine, which is now known as the Marengo Ridge. The remains of the moraine form the hills to the north and south of Marengo. At 1,051 feet above sea level, a hill located northeast of Marengo is one of the highest points in the state of Illinois. The valley, which became the setting for Marengo, was carved out of the large moraine by a post-glacial river flowing to the west. Today, as it was in the 1830s, the pristine waters of the Kishwaukee River, named in honor of Chief Big Thunder's daughter, flow through this beautiful valley. And just as their beauty beaconed to those early settlers in the fall of 1835, McHenry County's largest grove of sugar maple trees remain today to greet the traveler entering Marengo on East Grant Highway. It is no wonder that the early settlers called their new community Pleasant Grove. Disappointedly it was discovered that another Illinois community had already adopted the name Pleasant Grove. This resulted in the community being renamed Marengo in 1841.

As one becomes more familiar with the origins of Marengo's early settlers, time and again the states of Vermont and New York appear. These early families often had homes in other locations, like Ohio or Indiana, before coming west to Marengo. Some individuals, like A. B. Coon and Charles Robb, who observed and remembered the beauty, richness of natural resources, and well-situated location, returned after a short while to call Marengo their home for many generations.

It has been a great benefit to Marengo's historians to have access to the journals, family histories and memoirs of our early settlers. These sources tell of them following the Native American trails as they traveled westward. Many of these trails converged in the Marengo area. Some, like the Beldins, came, staked their claims, and returned to their previous homes for the winter. Still others had friends or relatives stake claims for them. Some, like William Sponable, were land speculators who sometimes improved their claims with log structures. It was an improved claim that the Sponables came to with six children, some of whom were sick. Christopher chose to purchase his brother William's speculative land, which had two log cabins already built and connected by a covered space.

Both the Beldin and Robb memoirs mention the helpfulness of the Native Americans. John Beldin, who staked his claim north of the Kishwaukee River on what would become River Road, recorded the following in his memoirs. "There was a big Indian Village [at Pleasant Grove]. Near our spring were several Indian families. They were the best neighbors I ever had. They were friendly and honest till the white man came and gave them whiskey. They supplied us with meat, venison, bear, etcetera and were delighted to get a little meal in return. They always gave us the best of the deal." Charles Robb, who originally settled near the Boone County line, and north of the Kishwaukee River, had this to say. "In those years [early 1840s], friendly Indians were a common sight. Their encampment was along the Kishwaukee River, which bordered [Charles's father] Alfred's farm on the south. The children played together."

There was a great fear of grass fires among those early settlers. These fires usually started as a result of lightning. Also striking fear in their hearts was the loss of a loved one. These early pioneers often had to make quick decisions to find suitable locations for family burials. Two early burial plots were in the vicinity of 535 East Grant Highway and 704 West Grant Highway. The Sponable graves were moved from West Grant Highway when the city cemetery was established on East Street. The Barber family plot on Hartman Road and the Storm plot on Maple Street experienced long periods of neglect, but have recently gained the attention of preservation and scout organizations. Many of the early Scottish residents of River Road are buried in the Scottish cemetery located on River Road. The cemetery was established on land provided by Alexander and Jane Stewart. It too went through periods of neglect, but descendents of the Wilson family have immaculately restored the grounds and researched the family history of its inhabitants.

Just how hard was the life of an early pioneer? Consider this passage from the memoirs of John Beldin:

We had just settled in (1836) on places to build our houses and were ready to go to work when I was taken sick. It was a sort of rheumatic fever and for days I lay helpless under a rude shelter that Ruben Tower (friend who accompanied John) built for me. He laid a pole from the branches of one tree to those of another. He thatched it by laying green brush on the north side, using brush with plenty of leaves, putting it on shingle fashion so it was wind and rain proof on the north but open on the south. Then he kept a fire burning in front so I was comfortably warm. One afternoon the cattle, one of which carried a bell, strayed away. Tower must go and hunt them. The afternoon wore away and he did not come back. In the southwest a terrible storm rose. However, the storm divided with the worst of it going north of me. My fire was nearly out and it was growing dark. I was too weak to mend my fire. To add to my discomfort and danger, wolves began to gather round snarling and crunching bones we had thrown out. I feared something had happened to Tower, some accident or mischance, that he would never return or if he did make his way toward me he would not be able to find me in the darkness. It was probably 2:30 or 3 a.m., the wolves were coming closer, growing bolder and bolder. It almost seemed as though I could feel their teeth meet in my flesh.

Suddenly, faint and far away, I heard the sound of the bell. I've heard lots of music since but none so sweet to me as the tinkle of that old cow bell.

From humble beginnings upon a Native American trail, the future town of Marengo prospered. The west was being settled, and Galena was often a destination through the fledgling village. As a result of these traveler's needs, Calvin Spencer kept the first public house in the area between 1835 and 1842. Perhaps, for the same reasons, Dr. Ward Burley Mason remained after he arrived in the winter of 1835–1836 to purchase a claim for Joseph Brayton. Mason was the first physician in the area. The first religious services were held in 1836. Woody Bailey is credited with opening the first store in 1835. The first schools were taught in 1835 by Carolyn Cobb and, in the winter of 1837–1838, by Orson P. Rogers. The first post office between Chicago and points west was established in Coral in 1837. Our first newspaper, the *Marengo Journal*, made its appearance in 1852. With the opening of the Galena and Chicago Union Rail line in 1852, the Marengo Collegiate Institute in 1856–1857, the First National Bank in 1871, the Reading Room is opened in 1882, preliminary to establishment of the library in 1907, McHenry County's first opera house in 1883, and by 1880, the establishment of five religious denominations were well established (Baptist, Catholic, German Lutheran, Methodist, and Presbyterian). This town became the most progressive in what became McHenry County.

Anson Rogers arrived in Marengo from Middletown, Vermont, in 1846–1847. His daughter, Maria Louise, married Ephraim H. Seward, also from Middletown, on November 5, 1846. Ephraim descended from an old Colonial family. His family was a branch of United States Secretary of State William H. Seward's family. William Seward was secretary of state under Pres. Andrew Johnson and is remembered for his part in the purchase of Alaska in 1867. At that time it was referred to as "Seward's folly." In the 1880s, Maria Louise Rogers Seward had this to say in a presentation to the Home Circle: "Although Marengo has not grown to be a great city and does not expect to be the world's metropolis, it has made a steady and wholesome advancement until it is one of the prettiest and most desirable resident towns in northern Illinois."

Business enterprise prospered, especially those associated with farmers and travelers. Because of the establishment of industries like the Collins and Burgie Stove Works in 1892, McGill's Manufacturing Company in 1924, and the Arnold Engineering Company in the 1930s, Marengo began the transition from a purely rural community to a community that acknowledged the financial stability of industrial employment.

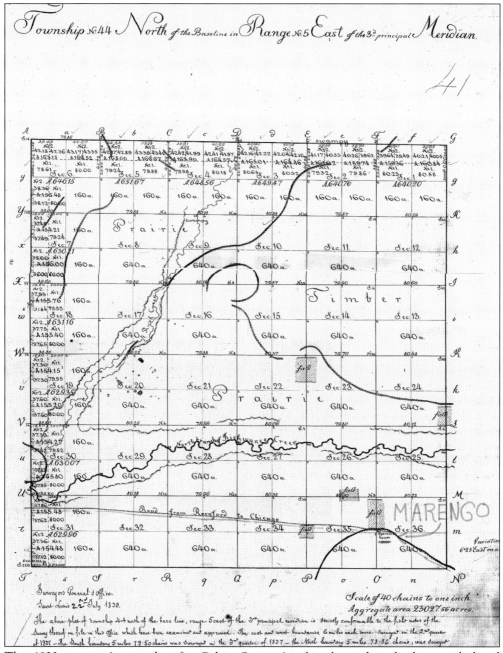

This 1830s surveyor's map identifies Calvin Spencer's cabin, located in the lower right-hand corner, on the Rockford-to-Chicago trail.

One

SETTLERS AND CITY FOUNDERS

Pleasant Grove was a welcomed sight to Maria Sponable and her family in the fall of 1835. It was pleasantly situated between two forests, and the soil was the finest they had ever seen, a rich, black loam. Her father, Christopher, purchased his brother William's 240-acre claim. Christopher built one of the first frame houses in Marengo. The Civil War greatly affected Maria's naturally happy disposition. Maria's entire family eagerly awaited word that the war would soon end. In April 1865, an anvil filled with gun powder exploded. A large piece of metal struck Harris Otis, leaving Maria a widow with four young children. She died of a "broken heart" in 1868 at the age of 39.

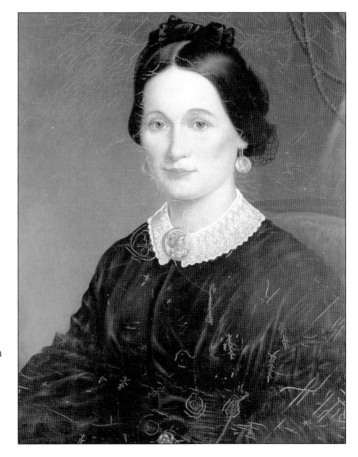

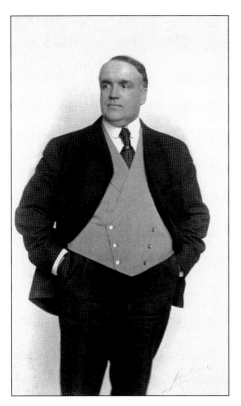

Ernest D. Patrick was born in Marengo in 1869 to Richard M. and Emma P. Patrick. After attending local schools, he studied at Lake Forest College and Phillips Exeter Academy in Exeter, New Hampshire. He married Leone Vail, daughter of prominent local residents Elisha and Delphi Vail. E. D., as he was commonly known, was a banker and was actively involved with the Collins and Burgie Stove Works.

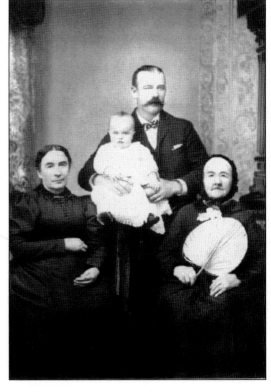

The current Deneen family of Marengo Township established its presence in the Marengo community in 1841 when John and Mary Hallisey settled on what remains the "family farm" on Hawthorne Road. Pictured are four generations, beginning with Mary Welch Hallisey (right), her daughter Hannah Hallisey Deneen (left), and Hannah's son William Deneen, who holds his son William Francis Deneen. (Courtesy of Mary Jane Deneen Bauman.)

At the death of his parents, Harris and Maria Sponable Otis, Stephen Otis was sent back to New York to be raised by relatives. As an adult, he returned to his place of birth, opening up a dry goods store at the corner of West Prairie and State Streets. He remained in business for 55 years, retiring in 1914. He was married to Jennie Warren Vandevere for 42 years.

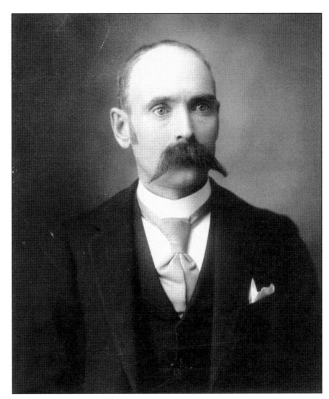

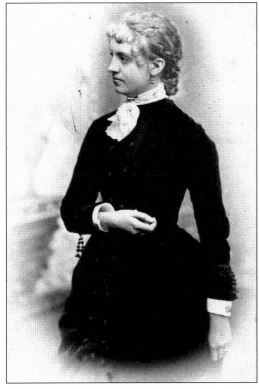

Alice Otis Burns was the daughter of longtime residents Harris G. and Alice Fillmore Otis. Her father owned the H. G. Otis Grocery for many years. Alice was the mother of well-known local physician Dr. Alice Mijanovich. (Courtesy of Alice Burns Mijanovich.)

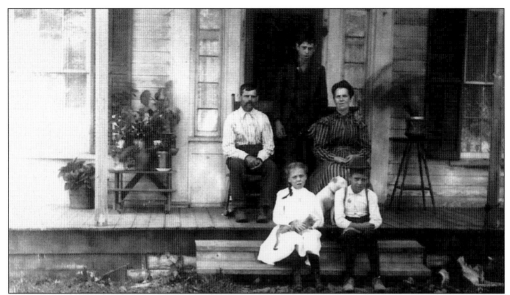

Pictured are Charles W. and Mabel Tidball Pope with two of their children, Betty and Albert. Standing is John Benton, son of their close friends. The Pope family lived on the Boise farm at 19923 East Grant Highway for many years. Note the always-present farm dog lying at the steps and the fern and flower pots sitting upon their stands. Their Greek Revival–style home was very popular in the early to mid-19th century. (Courtesy of Robert Pierce.)

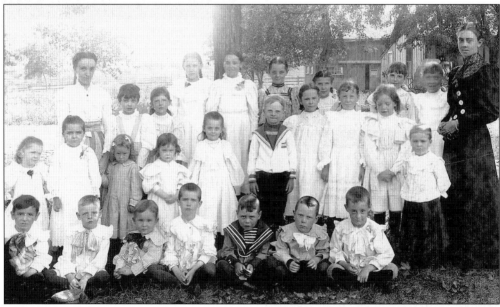

Only some of the names of these youngsters, dressed in their Sunday best, were recorded. They are, from left to right, (first row) Kenneth Woleben, John Fillmore, unidentified, Harry Patrick, and three unidentified; (second row) Lucille Sanders, Ada Curtis, Marjorie Swearinger, unidentified, Hazel Marks, Hal Otis, Wilma Jackson, unidentified, Henrietta Otis, and Clifford Dougherty; (third row) Lucy Smith Fry, Margrurite Vail, Helen Spencer, Bessie Sheldon, Marcia Crego, Ruth Barber, Mary Colver, Marie Seward, unidentified, and K. Barber Keiling. (Courtesy of Janice Patrick.)

Beginning in the later years of the 1800s, Tommy Gill began a long association with Steve Otis in the dry goods business. Gill maintained his own sideline business in musical instruments. Following the 1914 retirement of Otis, Gill ran his own jewelry store while continuing to provide for the interests and needs of local musicians.

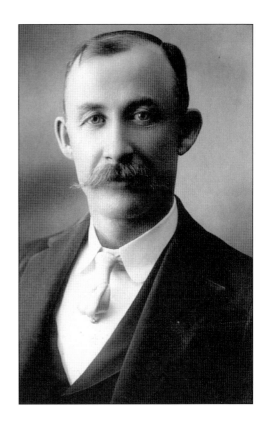

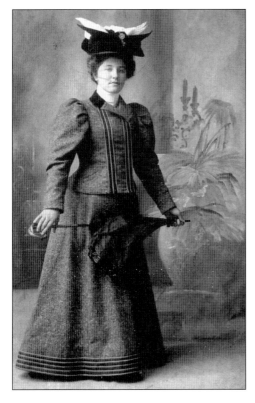

Married to nationally-known, big league ball player Carl Lundgren in 1904, Maude Cohoon Lundgren had a need to maintain an appropriate image. At that time, Carl was a pitching star of the National League Chicago Cubs. Just 30 years later, Maude held her husband's hand as he struggled to recover from a fatal heart attack. Maude eventually returned to her hometown of Marengo to live out her years. (Courtesy of Alice Burns Mijanovich.)

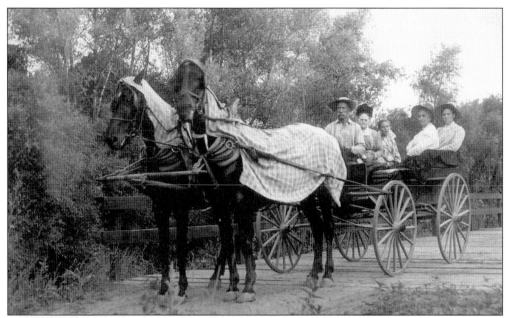

Even old Dobbin is cooperating by looking straight at the photographer. Pictured is the Daniel Peck family who lived on West Grant Highway, near the intersection with West Street. Daniel and his son Don were both employed for many years with the Bordens Milk plant on Sponable Street. Don Peck was the father of Richard Peck, owner of Peck's Jewelry. (Courtesy of Pamela Peck Woodruff.)

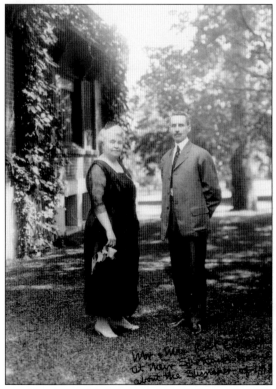

The Marengo Public Library was created by city ordinance on June 19, 1907. With sizable donations from Mrs. M. J. Harrington and the A. A. Ryder estate, locations were established in Dr. J. W. Green's residence and later in the office building of Dr. Frederick L. Nutt. In 1925, Harriet Otis initiated talks with Robert Strahorn for the construction of a memorial library. The result was the Strahorn Memorial Library, which was constructed by Andrew Lindquist for a total of $32,000. (Courtesy of Marengo Public Library.)

Herman Haas came to Marengo at the age of three in 1874. On November 4, 1903, he married Emma Trebes from Coral Township. She was a seamstress and made her own wedding dress. Herman worked at the Collins and Burgie Stove Works, Bordens Milk Plant, and later at McGills Metal Company. They lived many years at 519 East Washington Street. (Courtesy of Rodney Schaeffer.)

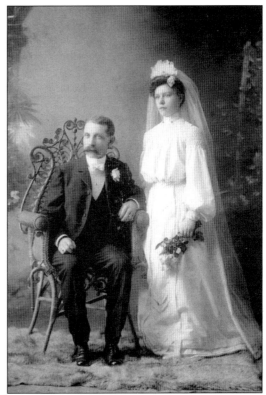

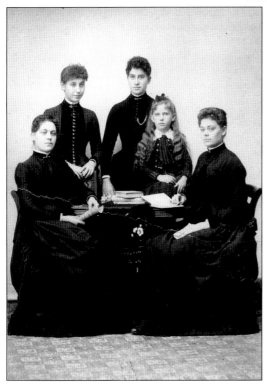

Sister bonds are strong for the Sisson sisters, from left to right, Anna Woleben, Lizzie Shurtleff, Belle Sears, unidentified, and Myrtle Cook.

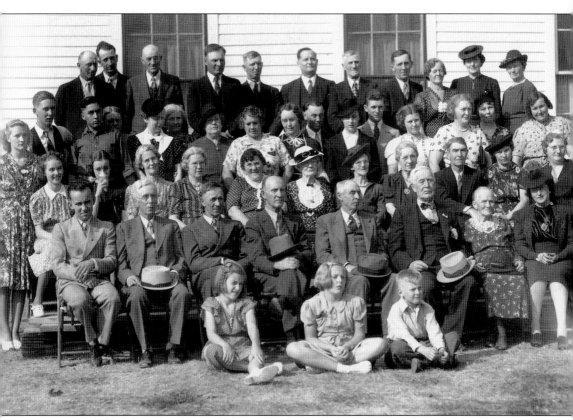

A Riley Township centennial celebration was held at the township hall in 1939. Pictured are descendents of many early Marengo area settlers. Included are, from left to right, (first row) Mavis Olcott; Arlene Anthony, and Wylie Anthony; (second row) Gardner Thomas; Earl Brotzman; Clyde Coarson; Lou Stockwell; Ralph Metcalf; Chet Grey; Emma Coarson, wife of Jonas Coarson; and Ollie Wilson, wife of Neil Wilson; (third row) Lily Medelberg; Violet Anderson Mallory; Merom Anthony, wife of Grant Anthony; Hildur Coarson, wife of Clyde Coarson; Esther Ruth, wife of August Ruth; Nell Griebel, wife of Fred Griebel; Rose Thompson, wife of Emory Thompson; Susan Diamond, wife of Tom Diamond; Tom Diamond; Hattie Mackey, wife of Burnice Mackey; and Ann Kraft, wife of Art Kraft; (fourth row) Irene Medelberg; Clarence Anthony; Howard Ruth; Ina Anthony, wife of Cleo Anthony; Johanna Westergren; Lil Griebel, wife of Roy Griebel; Ula Stockwell, wife of Lou Stockwell; Grace Johnson, wife of Carl Johnson; Helen Anderson, wife of Roy Anderson; Roy Anderson; Mildred Anderson Hubbs; Herb Sawallisch; Jeanette Mackey; Blenda Olcott, wife of Hugh Olcott; Mary Payne; and Mabel Shipman, wife of Clide Shipman; (fifth row) Gus Ruth; Walter Dahlman; Art Kraft; Henry Markison; Burnice Mackey; Rev. A. J. Bishop (Riley Methodist pastor); Grant Anthony; Cleo Anthony; Cora Furr, wife of Bill Furr; Ollie Nelson; and Ida Nelson. (Courtesy of Ethel Anthony.)

Marie Seward was the daughter of Frank and Clara Otis Seward, who were children of early settlers. Marie attended local schools, then graduated from Wellesley College. She was the granddaughter of Maria Louise Rogers and Ephraim Seward.

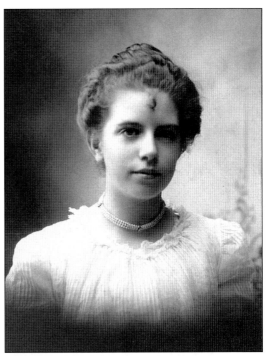

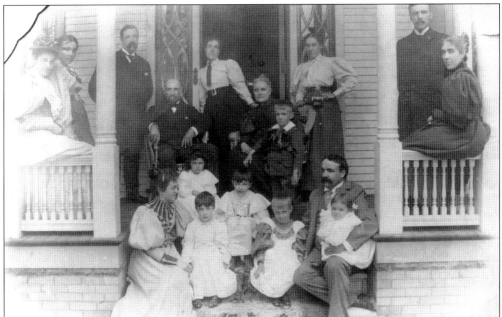

The Richard Montgomery Patrick family gathered in 1895 for a family picture at their residence, 327 West Prairie Street. From left to right are (first row) Leone Vail Patrick, wife of E. D. Patrick; Barbara Patrick; Isabelle Patrick; Marjorie Patrick; Marjorie Hillis; Ernest Durand (E. D.) Patrick; and Martha Patrick; (second row) Louise Cook Patrick, wife of Fred Albert Patrick; Rosamond Patrick; Fred Albert Patrick; Richard Montgomery (R. M.) Patrick; Frances Churchill Patrick; Emma Page Patrick, wife of R. M. Patrick; unidentified; Winifred Patrick; and Rev. Newell Dwight Hillis and his wife, Annie Patrick Hillis.

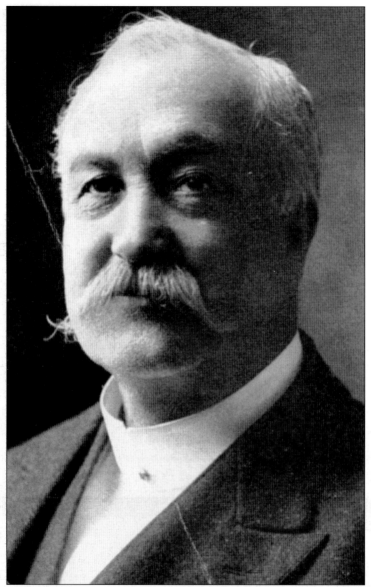

In 1861, Ira Curtiss and his mother arrived in Marengo from New York. Curtiss was a member of Company D, 15th Regiment, Illinois Volunteer Infantry, where he became a first lieutenant. During the last two years of the war, he was colonel of the 127th. Taken sick at Raleigh, Missouri, he was honorably discharged. He then accepted a clerkship in the provost marshal's office until the end of the war. Completing his study of law under Amos B. Coon, Curtiss was admitted to the bar. In 1876, he was elected state's attorney for McHenry County, serving eight years. He was the prosecutor for the first execution in the history of McHenry County. It was Curtiss who set the example, for the first time in the history of the county, of transferring all funds in the form of fines and forfeitures to the superintendent of schools. Curtiss served 15 years as attorney for the city of Marengo and was twice elected to the state legislature, first in 1870 as member of the House of Representatives and in 1884 as senator. He chaired various committees during this time. He received the honorary master of arts degree from his alma mater, Union College in New York in June 1890. (Courtesy of McHenry County Historical Society.)

Ira and Josie Curtiss were married May 27, 1874. Josie was an author of publications pertaining to health issues. For many summers, Josie brought boys out to the country from the Chicago slums to experience a healthier atmosphere. Adults provided the care and supervision, with the Marengo community helping to provide nutritious foods. Living accommodations were provided in the spacious barn at the rear of the property at 521 East Grant Highway. At the 1926 dedication of the new high school on East Grant Highway, Josie presented the deed to the home at 521 East Grant Highway to the board of directors in honor of her late husband, Hon. Ira Curtiss. For many years, the home was used as the residence for the high school principal. In the picture below, Ira and Josie are seated at each end of the third row. (Courtesy of McHenry County Historical Society.)

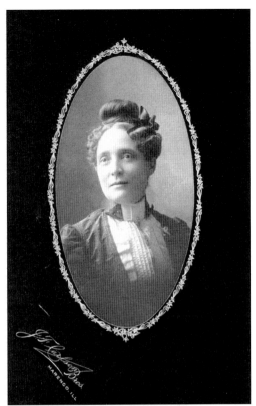

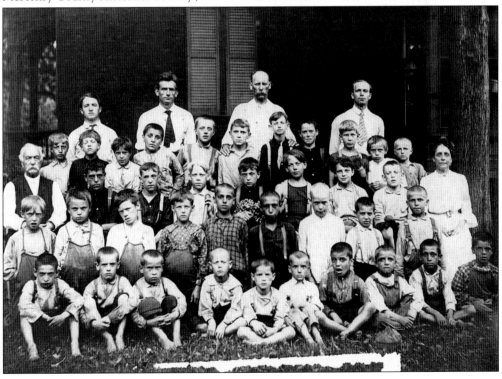

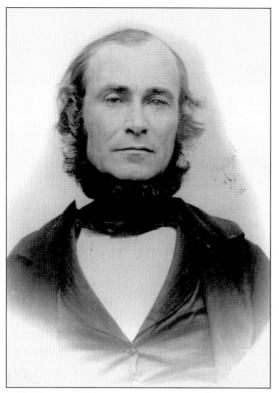

Amos B. Coon arrived in 1837 as a surveyor, platting out the original lots and blocks of Marengo. Shortly thereafter, he took up the study of law, rising to eminence at the bar as an able and successful lawyer. He became a leading counselor, versed in practical knowledge of the law, throughout McHenry County and the local congressional district. He prepared the charter for the incorporation of Marengo as a town in 1857. When he was 31 years old, and Harriet Damon just 17, Coon decided that he would settle for no less than to have Damon as his wife. Due to being mentally coerced into marriage, she lay near death for months, having to learn to walk and talk again. Based upon Harriet's memoirs, *Life and Labors of Auntie Coon*, Harriet came to personally know the power of God in her life. Members of Amos's family tried to keep the book from the public. (Courtesy of McHenry County Historical Society.)

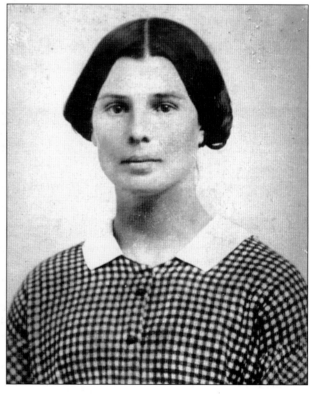

Two

EARLY MARENGO MEMORIES

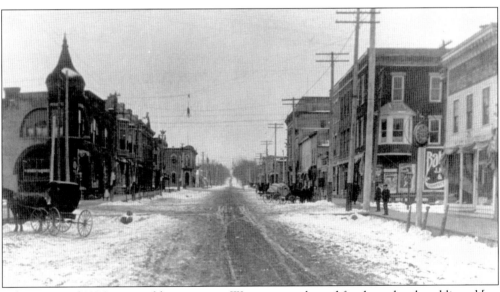

"The winter of 1936 was a cold, snowy one. We were snowbound for three days by a blizzard [on their farm near Kishwaukee Valley Road]. A rotary plow finally came through. It took three hours to get the four miles from Marengo," Mary Weaver said, according to *Ruminations, Reflections and Expectations*. From the same book, Raymond Deneen is quoted as saying, "I was six years old in 1913. Horse and buggy was the transportation used to attend religion classes and mass on Sundays. We could make it to town in 25 minutes [from Hawthorne Road]. In the spring the hard snow banks would thaw unevenly causing the cutter runners to sink into soft spots, tipping the sleigh and throwing the passengers onto the wet snow. There were runaways if the driver did not hang onto the reins!" Snow also affected State Street, as evidenced in this late-19th-century photograph. (Courtesy of Michael and Barbara Bigalke.)

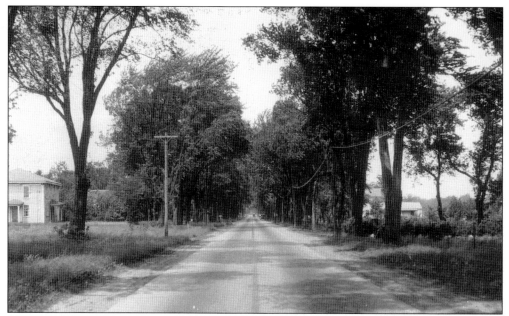

Christened Grant Highway in 1922 in honor of Pres. Ulysses S. Grant, this highway was touted in 1927 as going in a perfectly direct line from New York to Yellowstone Park. By 1930, this one-time stage route-immigrant trail would be known as the Atlantic-Yellowstone-Pacific Trail. This picture is from the 1920s, looking west on East Grant Highway from the area of 1081 East Grant. (Courtesy of Michael and Barbara Bigalke.)

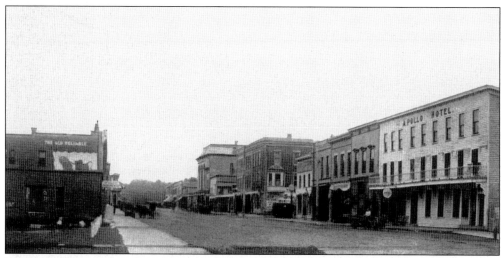

This early-20th-century photograph is of State Street, looking south. "I bought out Harry Ward's station [located on lower, right side of the Apollo Hotel] in 1932 for $300, lock, stock, barrel, accounts receivable, tools and products, all of which was in just a small niche on the north side of the old hotel. This included room for two pumps, almost in the sidewalk! I later bought and tore down the hotel and meat market. We used the lumber from the old hotel to build the [new] station," said Lawrence Perkins according to *Ruminations, Reflections and Expectations*. (Courtesy of Michael and Barbara Bigalke.)

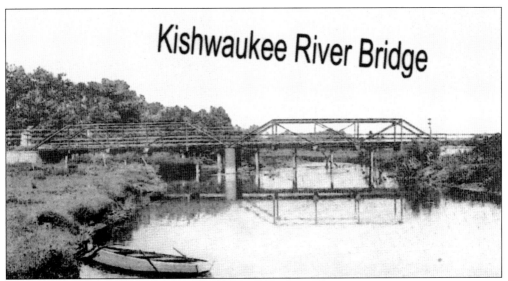

Kishwaukee River Bridge

The Native Americans called the Kishwaukee River *Kicki*, meaning creek. The pioneers named this creek-river Kishwaukee in honor of Chief Big Thunder's daughter. "There was more skating on the river when I was young. There used to be a great big, deep hole near where the [Smith] Mill used to be. It was a GREAT place to go fishing and swimming." Frank Woodruff is quoted as saying in *Ruminations, Reflections and Expectations*.

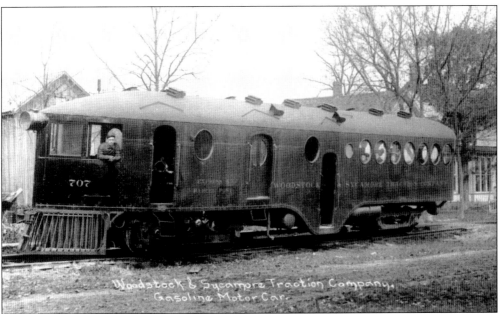

"One of my earliest memories [from 1910 to 1911] is of the street car that came down Main Street from Genoa. They called it the Prairie Schooner. It was run by a gasoline engine that was started by dropping a leadless shotgun shell into an iron thing on top of the engine. Then they would open this gate, pull the stirrer around and hit that thing with a rubber hammer," said Clifford Kitchen according to *Ruminations, Reflections and Expectations*. This is a photograph of streetcar No. 707.

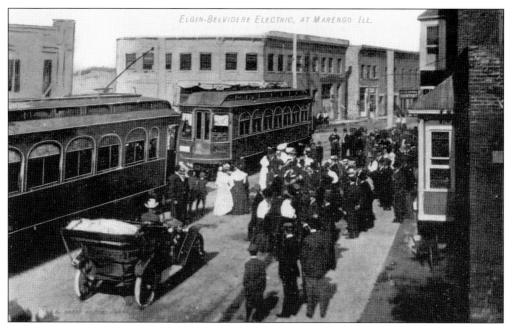

People gathered at the corner of West Prarie and State Streets to purchase their tickets. Walter Kehr is quoted in *Ruminations, Reflections and Expectations* as saying, "We came in to the German School on the Elgin-Belvidere street car. It came down East Prairie Street and stopped by the cemetery to let us off to walk to school. Sometimes there'd [also] be an 8 a.m. train on the North Western tracks. Those two would get into a race into Marengo! The old street car would out-shine the train!"

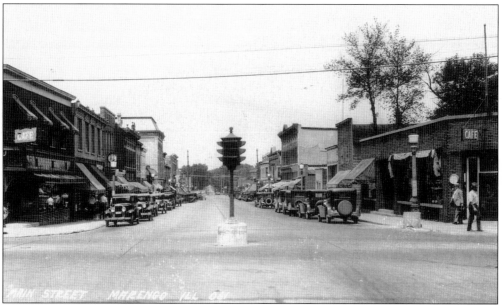

In the 1920s, as hard paving commenced on the former Galena Trail between Chicago and Rockford (then Route 5, now Route 20), the automobile industry boomed. It was at this time that Marengo gained its first traffic signal at the intersection of Routes 20 and 23. The signal was doomed in 1949 when it tangled with a truck. (Courtesy of Jeanette Mack Marks.)

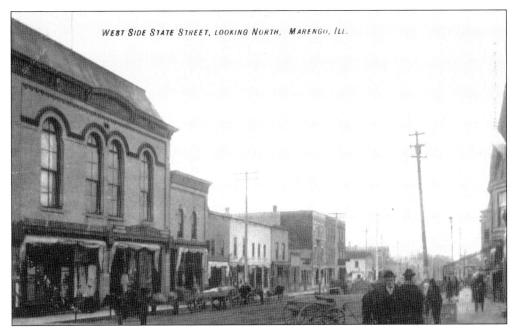

WEST SIDE STATE STREET, LOOKING NORTH. MARENGO, ILL.

Marengo was described by a writer on October 11, 1855, as follows: "Some of its early settlers remain but nineteen years have thinned their ranks and left but few who fought the first battles of Marengo over claims and claim lines, in the place where now are seen thronged streets, long lines of houses, shops, stores, churches and the stately uprising walls of the Marengo College." Shown here is State Street looking north. (Courtesy of Michael and Barbara Bigalke.)

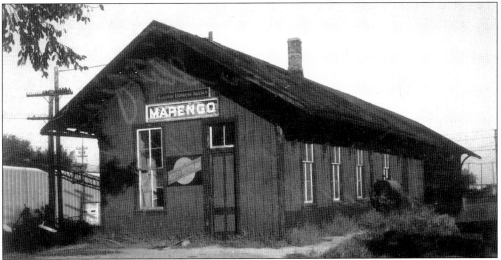

"We had an 8 a.m. train [passenger] that went to Chicago and two 10 a.m. trains that met here, one going each way, a milk train at noon that left empty cans and picked up full cars from the Borden plant at 6 p.m. At 6 p.m. two more trains met here, one going each way. The freight trains ran at various times, depending on need, I suppose. And then you sometimes had one going each way. We used to call it the 'try daily'—it would go up one day and try to get back the next!" Lawrence Perkins said according to *Ruminations, Reflections and Expectations*. This train depot is now in the Illinois Railway Museum in Union, Illinois. (Courtesy of Michael and Barbara Bigalke.)

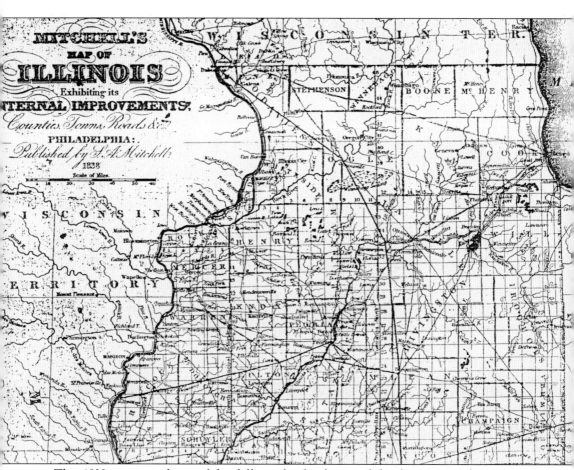

This 1838 map is evidence of the different levels of internal developments and improvements in the state of Illinois at that time. Note the fairly straight trail extending between the current locations of Chicago and Galena. This Native American trail led to Marengo, later becoming Grant Highway (U.S. Route 20). "As long as we benefit from the mistakes of other small communities which had a sudden influx of tremendous growth they couldn't handle, we can avoid the problems which could overwhelm our resources. I'm talking of city government furnishing such things as water, sewers, roads, gutters. Slower growth tends to eliminate some of the drains on the city. As long as things move along at a controllable pace, there won't be many insurmountable problems in the future," said Ralph Levin in *Ruminations, Reflections and Expectations.*

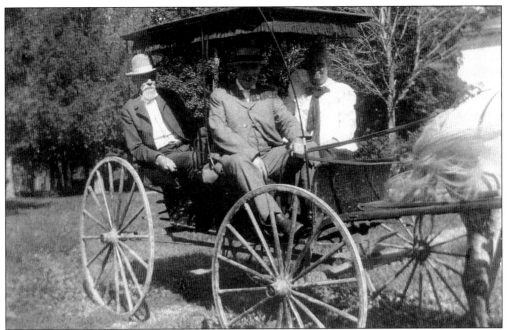

The Samuel Rowland family is going for a Sunday afternoon drive. Rowland purchased much of the former Christopher Sponable estate at 633 West Grant Highway in the early 1870s, moving the original Sponable home to Rowland Avenue and building the present home. Rowland was a Civil War veteran and ran a livestock business from his Maple Stock farm. He was the grandfather of Gladys Penney Miller.

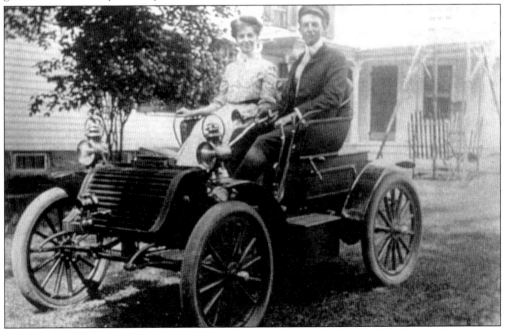

Cousins Ruth Sidwell and Ralph Beldin prepare to try out Beldin's fancy new automobile. This picture was taken in the yard of the Jacob Talbot residence at 739 South State Street, the grandparents of Ruth and Ralph.

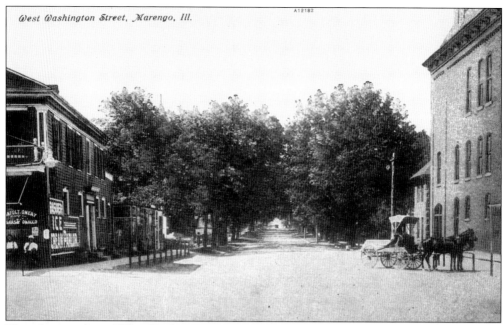

This photograph is of West Washington Street where Dr. Rozel Curtis built his home and office in 1906 on the corner of Ann and Washington Streets. Behind the building on the left was the office and home of Dr. Frederick Nutt. The elm trees in the background were fairly young, but one can see the beginnings of the gracious archway they eventually formed.

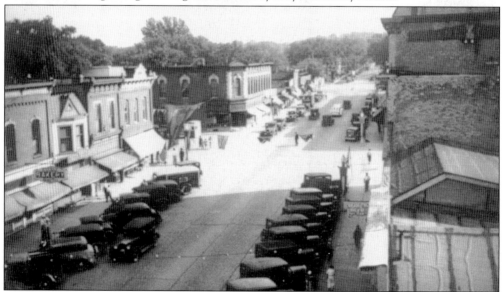

Harold Zenk brings this 1930s photograph of State Street to life with his recollections. "My Uncle Joe (Zenk) was something of a character, rather excitable! The guys would get together over at Max Wilson's Poultry shop and figure out ways to heckle him! They'd pull stunts like putting a sign in his window, 'Free Haircuts Thursday.' Pink Arlington was always pulling tricks on everyone. Pink used to say 'when I'm pushing up the daises, I'm gonna sit right up and say, I had a "heck" of a good time!'" accounted Harold Zenk in *Ruminations, Reflections and Expectations*. (Courtesy of Frank J. Mack family.)

Three

HISTORIC HOMES

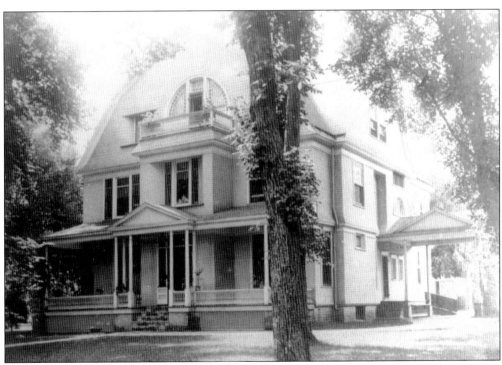

The Richard M. Patrick home was situated in a large, beautiful park setting. The interior was fitted with the modern conveniences of the late 1880s, lighted by gas and electricity. "There were six fireplaces in the house and the white marble one upstairs was always our favorite. When you came in the front door, the living room was to the left, and to the right was the library. From the living room you went through a large open doorway to the dining room, and from there, were great big sliding doors that opened into the rear of the front hall. The third floor was a ballroom. It had wood walls and a real nice floor, and balconies to the north and east. There was a big water tank up on the third floor that gravity fed any plumbing in the house," recollected Ethel Bauman Anthony according to *Ruminations, Reflections and Expectations.*

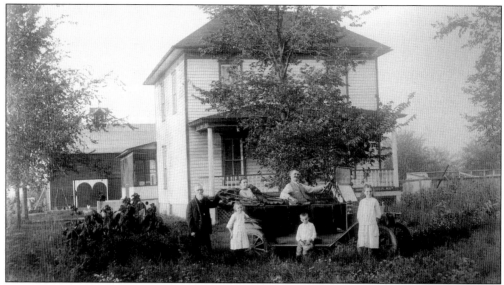

For many years, this was the farm home for the Lee Grover family. It is the first farmstead west of Ritz Road. At the death of Clinton Grover, Lee Grover's son, the home and associated farm buildings were sold. (Courtesy of Glenda Jones Hughes.)

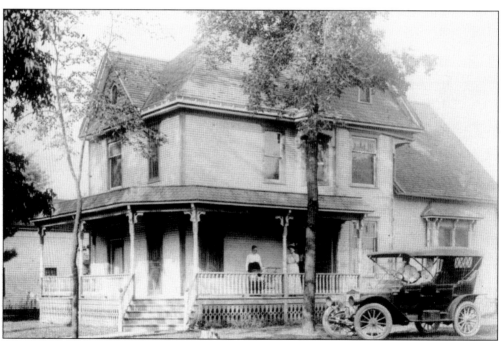

This home at 213 North Taylor Street was built in 1898 by the Charles Carpenter family, grandparents of Alice Colver. Good fortune and good health enabled them to celebrate their golden anniversary in their home. Charles conducted a feed business from his spacious garage, located on the property. (Courtesy Michael and Barbara Bigalke.)

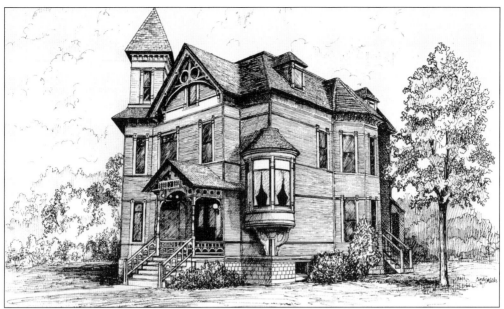

Francis Wayland Patrick was the nephew of Richard M. Patrick. Francis was prominently associated with the Marengo Creamery and Sugar of Milk Company, incorporated in 1898. The company annually turned out 75,000 pounds of butter, 75,000 pounds of cheese, 500,000 pounds of sizing, and 600,000 pounds of sugar, with shipments made through their New York agents. In the early 1900s, this company was one of only three in the United States. Their products took the name of Marengo all over the world. George Garnsey was the architect for Francis Wayland and Harriet Vandevere Patrick's Eastlake/Queen Anne–style home, built in 1885–1886 at 321 East Washington Street. Before their marriage, Harriet was a telegraph operator in Marengo. They were the parents of Howard and Harry Patrick. Harry's wife, Helen, was a longtime music teacher and First Baptist church choir director. (Above, courtesy of Cindy Miller Design; below, courtesy of Janice Patrick.)

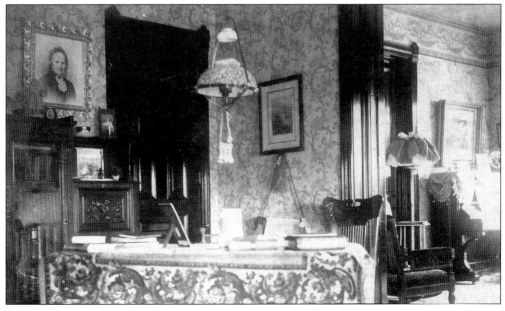

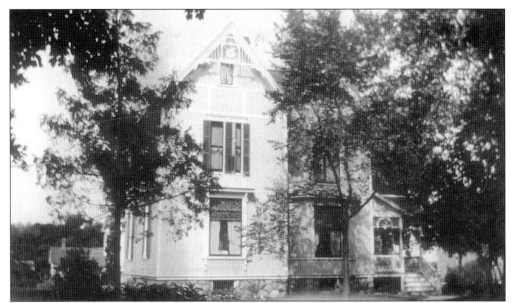

As a result of this home, at 658 East Grant Highway, being pictured on a Kellogg's cereal box, it is often referred to in recent times as the "Kellogg House." This 1926 picture was taken by the Church family who lived there at that time. (Courtesy of Leona Church Wilkening.)

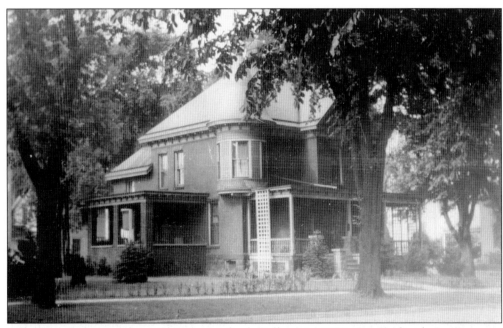

Following graduation from Chicago Medical College in 1878, Dr. Frederick L. Nutt was associated with Marengo doctor J. W. Green. He built this beautiful redbrick home at 123 West Washington Street. Stephen W. Otis purchased the home in the 1930s, living there until the 1960s. The home was sold to the owners of Wisteds Grocery, Pecks Jewelry and Levins Dry Goods, who tore the home down for a parking lot.

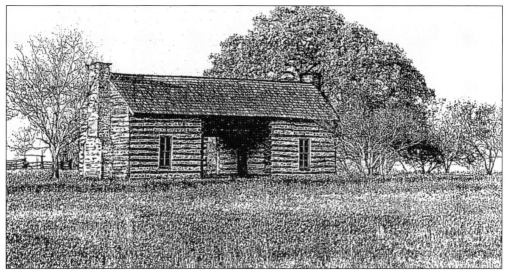

William Sponable arrived in the fall of 1835, speculating on 240 acres along the Galena Trail (U.S. Route 20). He improved the claim by building two connected log cabins as depicted in the photograph, selling this claim to his brother Christopher, who arrived with his family in the fall of 1836. Approximately four years later, Christopher built a Greek revival home for his growing family on the site at 633 West Grant Highway.

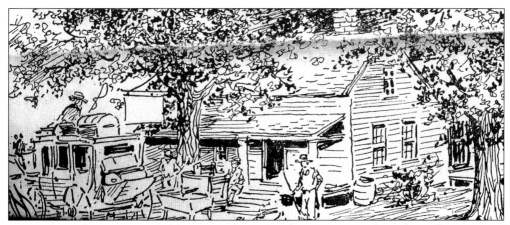

Drawn from descriptions of old-time residents, local artist Ray Walters drew this image of Calvin Spencer's original home at the corner of State Street and Grant Highway for Marengo's centennial edition of the *Marengo Republican News*. Spencer was Marengo's official original settler. The home served as a stopover for the many weary travelers on the trail to Galena.

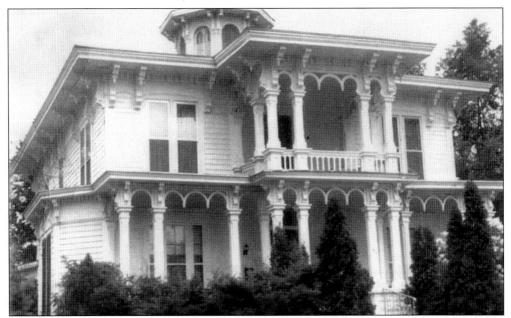

Purchasing seven acres from Christopher Sponable, Charles and Jane Marie Osborne Hibbard built this home at 413 West Grant Highway around 1846. There are 14 rooms in the home with a circular stairway and an octagonal shaped cupola. It is an accepted fact that the home was used as a safe stop for runaway slaves. The home is an exact replica of Hibbard's childhood home. Hibbard moved to Marengo from Charleston, South Carolina.

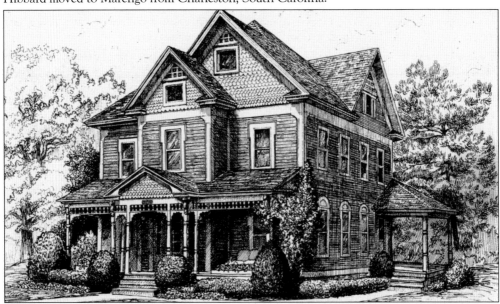

It appears that Eugene F. McKinney built this home at 406 West Prairie Street in the late 1860s. McKinney was in the mercantile business with C. W. Ingersoll. McKinney also had a canning business. Abner and Caroline Kelley lived in the home between 1894 and 1945. Abner and his brother, Alexander James, were associated in their father's foundry business on West Railroad Street. In 1906, Abner started the first Ford dealership in McHenry County. (Courtesy of Cindy Miller Design.)

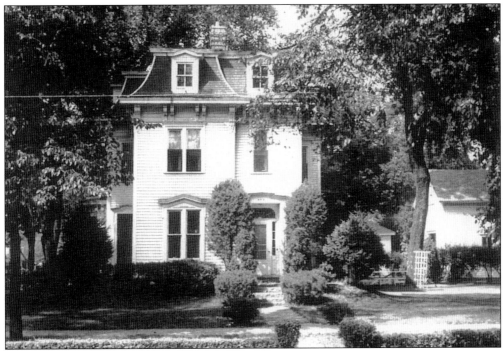

"I wasn't quite five at the time my parents purchased [the property at] 304 E. Washington Street. After many weeks of renovation the house was done and we moved in, in the fall of 1931. It was so BIG. My bedroom was upstairs while mother and father slept in the downstairs bedroom. I was having none of that! For a number of months my crib was in the corner of my parent's room where it was SAFE!" This quote is from Trudy Robb Yates's memoirs.

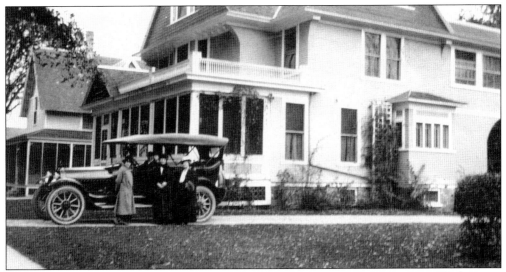

Ernest Durand and Leone Vail Patrick chose to build their home at 408 West Washington Street, just behind the home of his parents, Richard Montgomery and Emma Patrick at 327 West Prairie Street. E. D., as he was called, served as mayor of Marengo and as township supervisor. He had a very credible reputation. Their home was remodeled around 1950, when the Tudor-style stucco was added. (Courtesy of McHenry County Historical Society.)

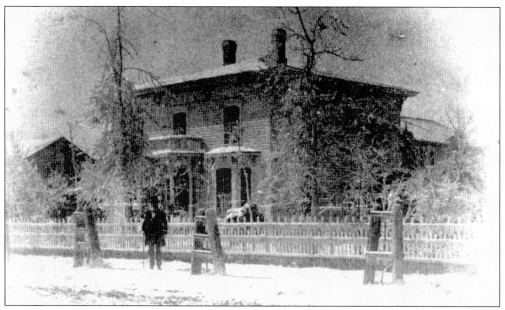

This home at 320 South State Street is one of the many landmark homes in Marengo. Built in the late 1840s to early 1850s for attorney Amos B. Coon, it remained in the ownership of the Coon family over 100 years. Amos and Harriet Coon's son, Adelbert, was a well-known band leader. His wife, Carolyn, was also a talented musician, providing early instruction to local composer Egbert VanAlstyne.

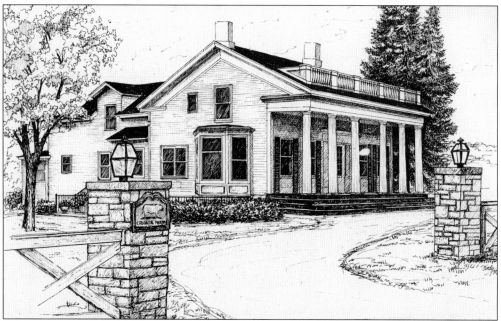

Anson and Rebecca Hart Rogers built this home in 1846–1847. It is one of the many old landmark homes located on Grant Highway. Anson hauled the lumber and Grecian columns for the home from Chicago. The trim for the home was made by hand from local lumber. Following the Rogers' death, the property was left to their daughter and her husband, Maria Louise and Ephraim Seward. (Courtesy of Cindy Miller Design.)

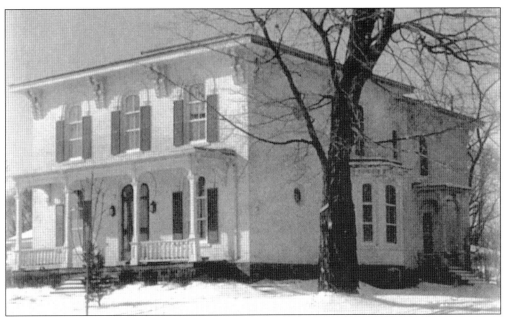

No matter how one looks at his name, it is Nebelow V. Woleben, forwards and backwards! Born in Marengo in 1860, he earned an honorable reputation based upon his business principles. He began with the First National Bank and in the 1890s, was managing partner of Woleben and Patrick's Dry Goods and Clothing. Nebelow and Frances Marsh Woleben had eight children. The Woleben family's "home on the hill," pictured above, was the location for many community gatherings.

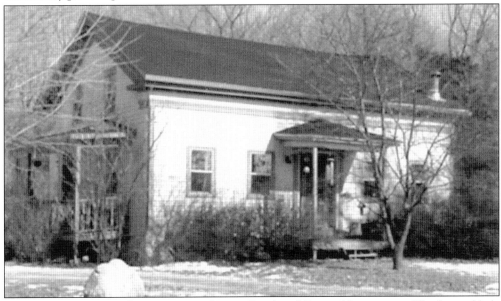

This home, at the northwest corner of River Road and Route 23, is a gem. The home likely was built around 1845 by either Harriet Damen Coon's father or by J. Hutchison. It became known locally as the Hutchison Farm. Hutchison's son, John N., was called to the pastorate of the Marengo Presbyterian Church in 1875. In the early years, there were many of these Greek Revival–style homes located on River Road.

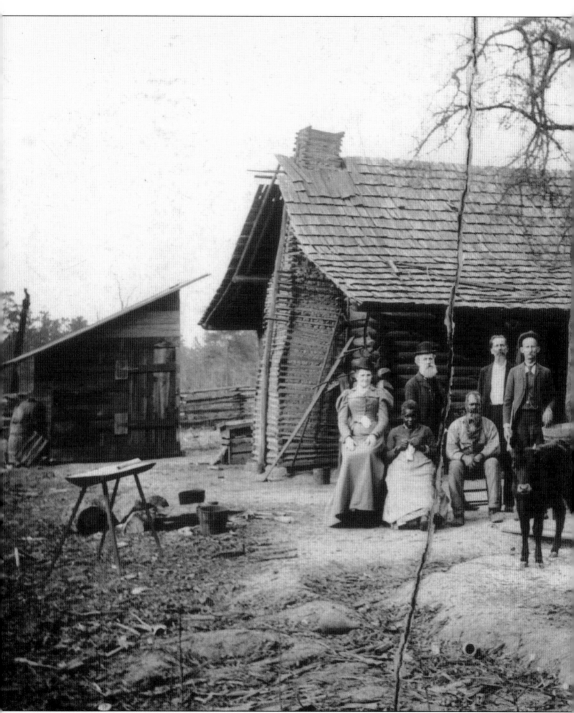

The reason for this early-20th-century gathering at the cabin home of Mr. and Mrs. John (Jack) Ford, at the corner of Forest and Dietz Streets, is unknown. The Fords are seated to the left in the picture. Jack was employed by the J. H. Patterson Company. Those attending and the food they provided include the following: Mrs. Charles Strickland, three quarts of pickles; Mrs. J. T. Beldin, five quarts of corn; Mrs. Frank Loomis, one white cake, two loaves of bread;

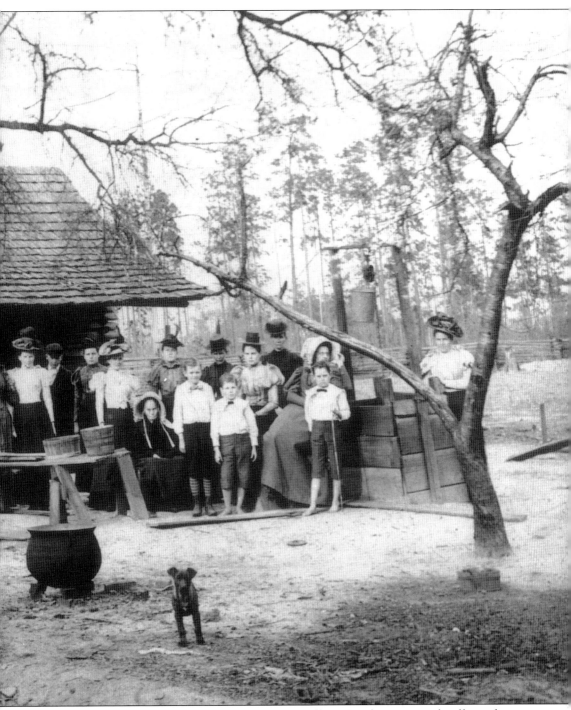

Mrs. D. Morris, two dozen white sandwiches; Mrs. William Casely, one pound coffee and sugar; Mrs. Moses Dimon, five dozen sandwiches; Mrs. Daniel Boyington, white cake and three quarts corn; Mrs. C. P. Fillmore, white cake; Mrs. M. E. Bushaw, Mrs. Wallace, and Mrs. Samuel Rowland, meats, bread, butter, and sandwiches; and Mrs. Al London, two loaves brown bread.

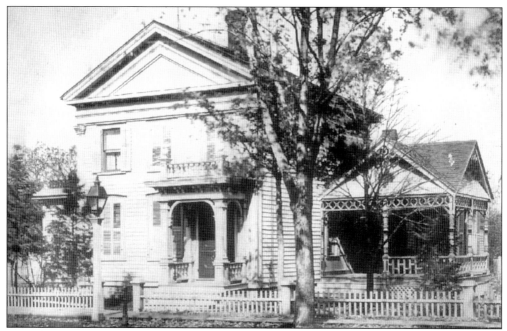

As a child in the 1930s, Dr. Alice Burns Mijanovich did not have far to go when visiting her maternal grandparents and great-grandparents. Charles and Harriet Alice Fillmore lived in this home at 514 East Washington Street. Harris and Alice Fillmore Otis lived right next door, at 502 East Washington Street.

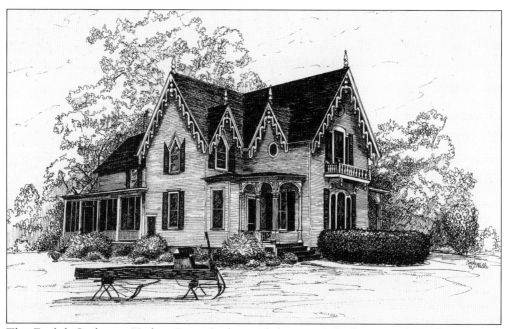

This English Gothic, or Hudson River Gothic–style home, was built in 1872 by Seth Lewis. But it is the Bartholomew and Crissey families who are commonly associated with the home, owning and living there for about 75 years. Photographs of the Crissey family business are included in this Marengo history publication. (Courtesy of Cindy Miller Design.)

Four

EARLY ENTERPRISES

The Collins and Burgie Stove Factory was built in 1892 as a result of generous financial contributions by Marengo's leading citizens. Located at the south end of what is now Zion Lutheran athletic field, it was two stories high and covered more than 100,000 square feet. Railroad tracks ran along two sides of the building, enabling the unloading of raw materials, plus the loading of the factory's products, mainly Leader stoves and ranges. It employed an average of 100 to 150 men. The company had started in Chicago in 1857. The factory was destroyed by fire in 1907 and never rebuilt. (Courtesy of McHenry County Historical Society.)

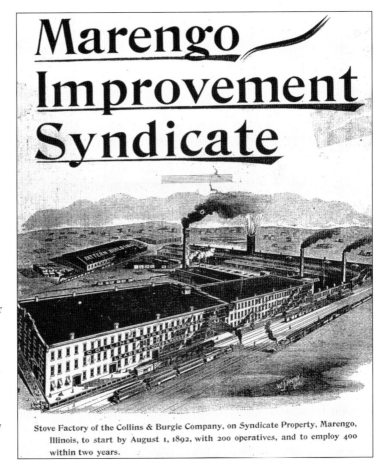

Stove Factory of the Collins & Burgie Company, on Syndicate Property, Marengo, Illinois, to start by August 1, 1892, with 200 operatives, and to employ 400 within two years.

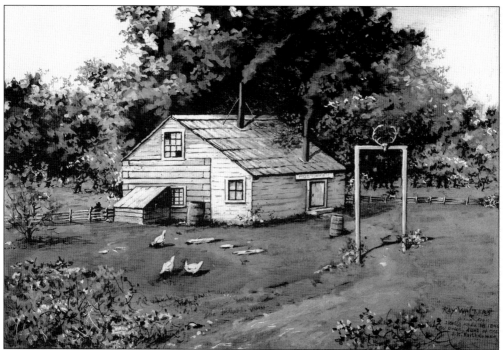

Sitting in front of the log cabin in 1840, S. K. Bartholomew's aunt, Mrs. Owen, drew the original sketch of the Buckhorn Tavern. It was located in Coral on the site of the Potawatomi Indians' dance grounds. Built by Proctor Smith in 1835, it served as a post office, hotel, and gathering location. It was the first post office between Chicago and Galena. The sketch shown was redrawn by Ray Walters in 1935 from Owen's original sketch.

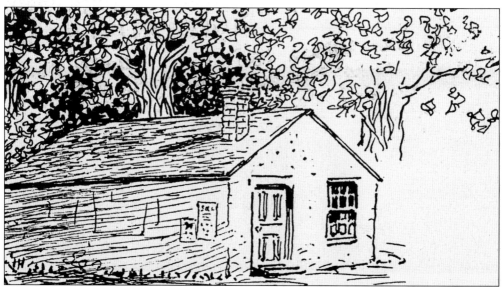

The "old Mud Store" was a favorite and a point of pride among the early settlers. It sat at the intersection of the old Native American trail (Grant Highway) and State Street. Built by M. G. Stevens in the 1840s, it served many different purposes, from a post office to a poultry shop. It was torn down in 1896.

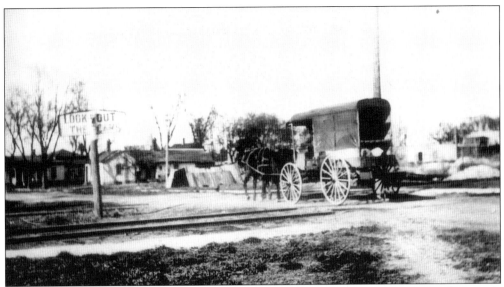

It would be nice to have milk delivered to the door once again. Ralph Curtiss is heading north on Taylor Street, making his deliveries. (Courtesy of Michael and Barbara Bigalke.)

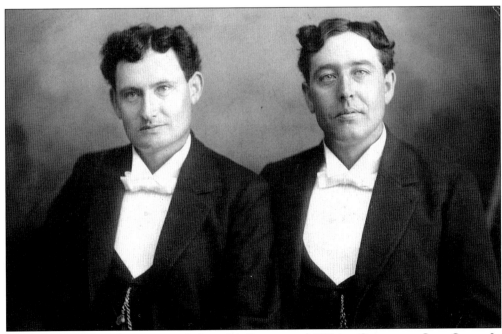

The 1877 McHenry County records list a McGovern and O'Brien Grocery on State Street. In the 1920s, the building was referred to in newspapers as the McGovern Block. Frances (left) and James McGovern were proprietors of the McGovern Tavern at 200 South State Street. There were living quarters on the upper floor. James and his wife, Anna, are the grandparents of Barbara McGovern Bigalke. (Courtesy of Barbara McGovern Bigalke.)

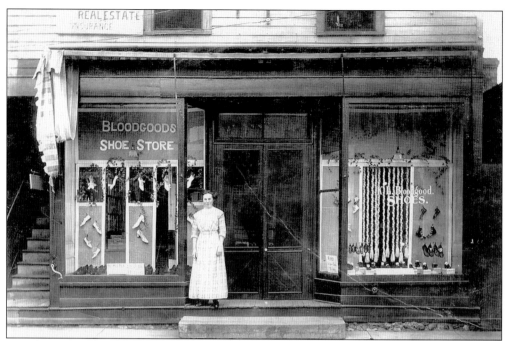

Following the death of her parents, Kate Bloodgood ran the Bloodgood shoe shop at 110 South State Street, the current location of the Marengo Café. She was one of many successful women entrepreneurs of the late 1800s and early 1900s. The family lived at 642 East Washington Street.

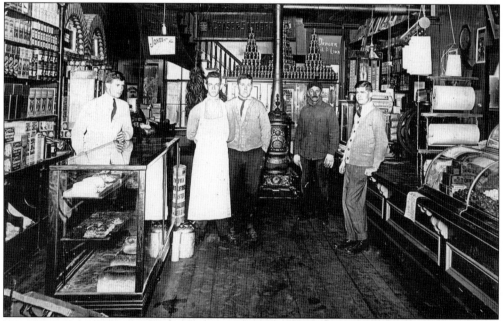

Harry and Howard Patrick were the sons of F. Wayland and Harriet Vandevere Patrick. The brothers founded the Patrick Brothers Grocery in 1906. In 1934, Harry bought out Howard's interest, and in 1935, Harold Feiertag and Milo H. Kuecker purchased an interest in the store. Harry Patrick stands at the far right. Howard stands behind the counter. The others are unidentified. (Courtesy of Janice Patrick.)

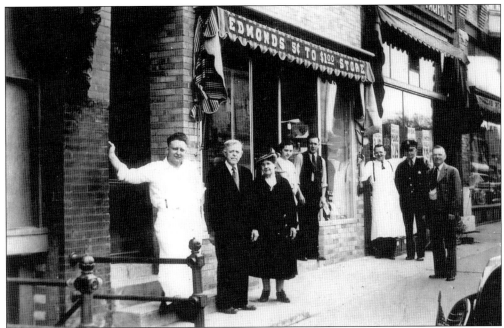

"I worked at Mr. Edmond's variety store in the 1940's. Mr. Edmonds' store was in the middle of the building at 100–105 South State Street. Guse's tavern was to the north, the A&P grocery to the south. Items available for sale included wearing apparel, housewares, stationary, school supplies, and toys. There also was a candy counter and a place for seasonal items, like fireworks." This quote is from Helen Haas Hess. Seen in the photograph, Harold Guse is on the left, and Helen Haas is fourth from left. (Courtesy of Helen Haas Hess.)

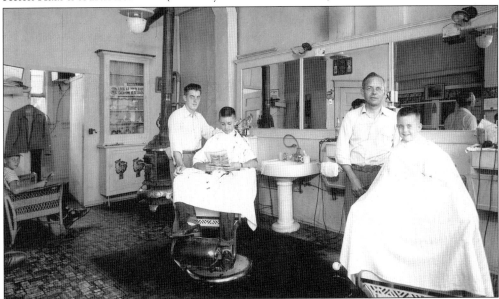

This image is almost like a scene right out of the televisions Mayberry. The location is Wolf's Barber Shop at 222 South State Street. From the left, sitting in a chair reading a comic book, is Charlie Naugle. Barber Bob Hills is cutting Rodney Schaeffer's hair while Terry Schaeffer is getting a similar cut from barber Harry Wolf Sr. (Courtesy of David Wolf.)

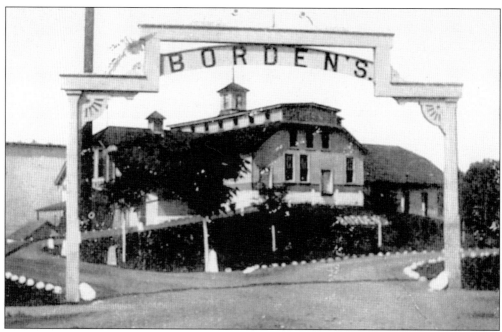

February 17, 1914, "Today we started our ice at Bordens. The ice is about 9 or 10 inches thick." February 28, "Last night we got a strong wind from the west and it started to snow and blow. I helped on the ice from 7 to 10. It is real cold again and I believe that they will get the old ice house full before it starts to thaw. We are still making butter." March 7, "Two hours before quitting time, the ice chute broke and a Hollander fell and both his legs were broke. He was sent to Elgin to be cared for." April 10, 1916, "The farmers did not bring their milk, for they were all on a strike for $1.55 (per hundred pounds of milk). The average Borden pays is $1.35. Well, early in the morning the crossings were packed with farmers. No one was allowed to take a drop of milk to the factory. Fred Zickuhr made an attempt to go through the bunch and refused to take his milk back home so all his milk was dumped into the road." These quotes come from the journal of Herman Haas. (Above, courtesy of Michael and Barbara Bigalke; below, courtesy of Pam Woodruff.)

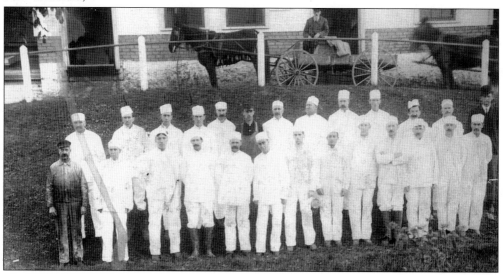

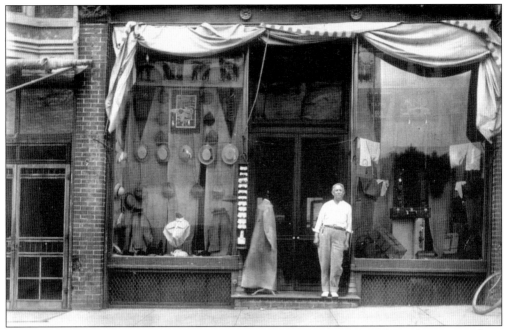

George Samter arrived in Marengo in 1859, becoming a highly respected merchant not only in Marengo but throughout McHenry County. Dealing in men's and children's clothing as well as associated amenities, he was associated with a number of stores throughout the country. By purchasing in large quantities, he kept his prices low. The business became known as "the old reliable," continuing in business for many years. (Courtesy of Michael and Barbara Bigalke.)

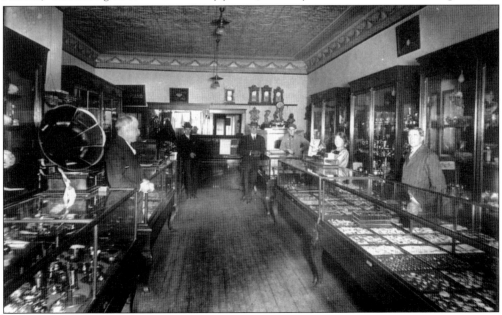

Starting in the general merchandise business with Stephen Otis in the late 1800s, Tommy Gill continued his State Street presence following Otis's retirement. This picture includes Tommy Gill, G. H. Rogers, Alice O'Cock, Mr. Atwood from the Gorham Company, George Perryman, and Ira J. Gill. (Courtesy of Michael and Barbara Bigalke.)

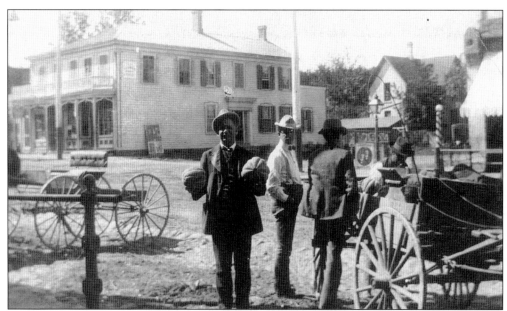

Look at the size of those melons! One can only expect to see the wagon filled with home-grown produce. The large building with the double-deck porch was located at the corner of West Washington and State Streets. It had living quarters on the second floor. Richard Montgomery and Emma Patrick lived here following their marriage in 1856. (Courtesy of Michael and Barbara Bigalke.)

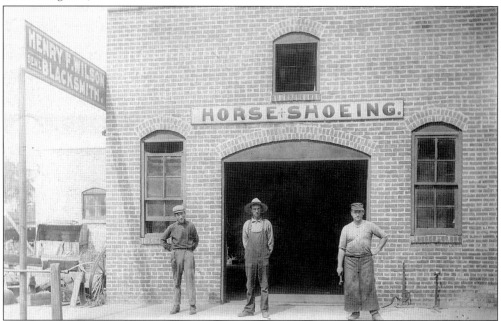

Third-generation blacksmith Bill Wilson is standing to the left. His father, Henry Forest Wilson, stands to the far right in front of their shop, located just south of the intersection of East Prairie and Taylor Streets. Bill's grandfather, Miles Grennon, started the family business profession about a block away on Prairie Street. Grennon was a horseshoer and wheelwright in the Civil War. He was a pallbearer at Pres. Abraham Lincoln's funeral. (Courtesy of Pat Marsh Church.)

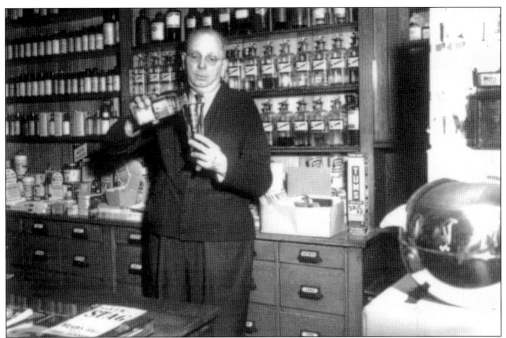

Pharmacist Arlie Shearer was a familiar sight to Marengo residents through the years of 1930 through the 1960s. Born in 1896 to Riley farmers Henry and Fannie Shearer, Arlie graduated from the University of Wisconsin School of Pharmacy in 1924, opening Shearer Pharmacy soon after. He was a World War I veteran. (Courtesy of Michael and Barbara Bigalke.)

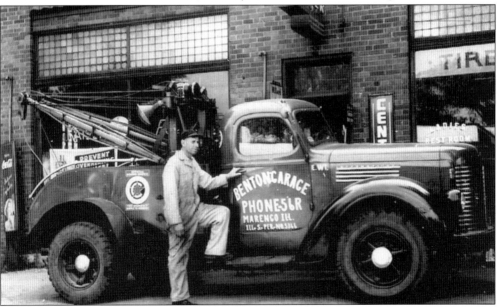

Beloved for his gentle and generous ways, John Benton is shown here in front of his Kaiser and Frazer automobile dealership and repair shop at 201 East Grant Highway. "Johnny was *one* of the most dedicated citizens to ever live in this city I believe. He saw that the flags were out on the streets every Memorial and holiday," remembers Adin Slaughter in *Ruminations, Reflections and Expectations*. (Courtesy of Barbara Koplin.)

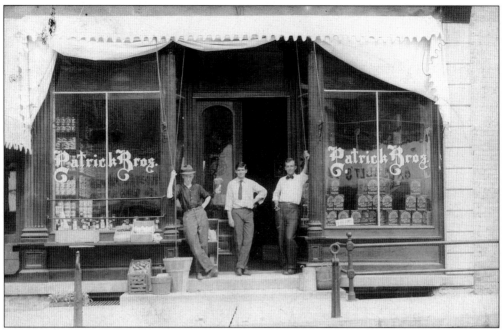

Harry and Howard Patrick stand to the right in the doorway of the Patrick Brothers Grocery at 127 South State Street. During the early 1900s, the clearly identifiable hitching posts were a necessity as were the side-street livery stables and tie barns. In 1915, the brothers built a new and larger store at 200 South State Street. (Courtesy of Marengo Public Library.)

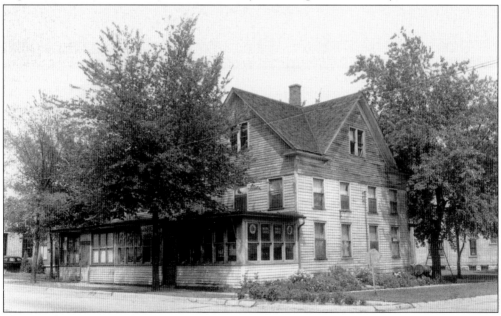

This building at the northwest corner of Taylor Street and Route 20 served as a home, a grocery store, and in 1943, as the first location of Bobby Carroccia's shoe shop. "Someone told me that Marengo needed a shoemaker, so that's why I came here. Every day I hitch-hiked back and forth to Rockford. There were no houses to rent in Marengo," said Bobby Carroccia in *Ruminations, Reflections and Expectations*. (Courtesy of Frank J. Mack family.)

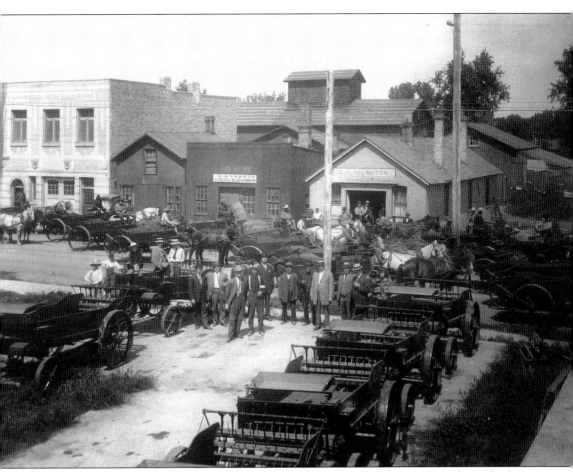

In the early 1900s, the southwest corner of Taylor and East Prairie Streets was used as a display area for new machinery. The machinery would then be auctioned off. Men identified in the foreground are Earl Penney (wearing straw hat), Henry Hauschildt (with suspenders), August Luhring, Newt Robb, and Chris Bremer. City hall is to the left in the photograph, with the Hance Woodworking and Sandman/Arlington Blacksmith Shop to its right. To the rear of these buildings are the Sullivan Brother's horse barns. This vacant lot previously was the location of a livery stable, but it burned down, killing 23 horses.

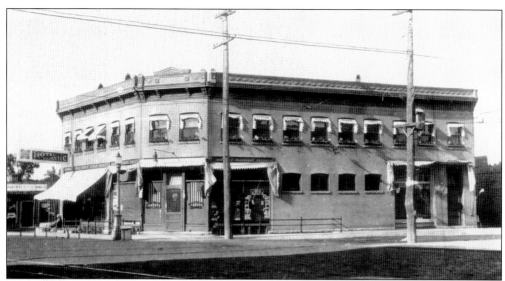

The Majestic Hotel occupied the second floor and the Triangle Grocery the first floor in the 1940s. "Twice a week the Triangle Grocery truck arrived at our farm. If we could get three loaves of bread for a dozen eggs, it was very good. A person was fortunate during the war to be a regular customer in one of the grocery stores. Sometimes the owner would put scarce items, such as chocolate, raisins or coffee, under the counter for his steady customers," relates Mary Beldin Weaver according to *Ruminations, Reflections and Expectations*.

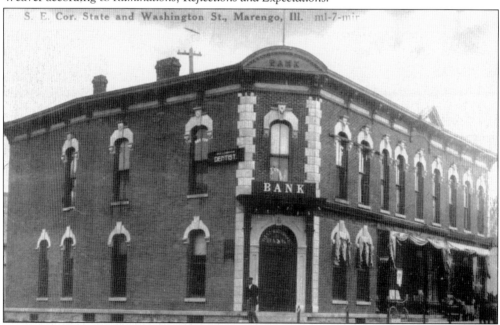

Marengo's banking history started with the private bank of Richard Montgomery Patrick. The First National Bank was incorporated in 1871, with Patrick as its president. Located on the southeast corner of State and East Washington Streets, the First National Bank was the first bank in McHenry County. First National had a capital and surplus of $75,000, with deposits of $220,000. Nebelow V. Woleben served as a cashier in the 1880s. (Courtesy of Michael and Barbara Bigalke.)

Ernest Robb was born in Riley Township in 1878 to Charles and Emogene Axtel Robb. As soon as he was old enough to "sit a saddle," Ernest went with his father and brother to herd cattle to his father's stockyards in Marengo. He was one of the first employees hired by Bordens in 1903, and in 1913, was superintendent of the company. In his retirement, he took up the insurance business. (Courtesy of Michael and Barbara Bigalke.)

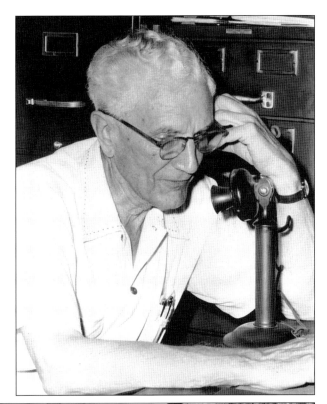

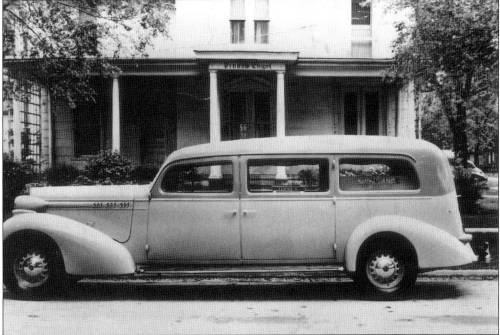

Long before the rescue squad formed, the local undertakers provided ambulance service for local residents. Pictured in front of the Pinnow Funeral Home, is this early-1940s ambulance. Edward and Edna Pinnow purchased the home from Charles Higbee. (Courtesy of Shirley Pinnow Kitchen.)

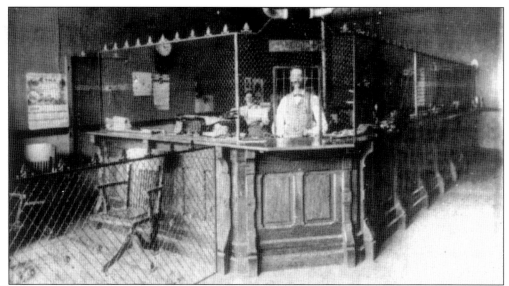

The Dairyman's State Bank was founded November 1, 1890, by prominent local businessmen I. R. Curtiss, W. Dougherty, W. W. Joslyn, S. B. Gardner, I. N. Muzzy, A. A. Ryder, A. S. Norton, L. Woodard, and J. E. Williams. Former senator Hon. I. R. Curtiss was named president, and L. Woodard, vice president. Dairyman's had an original capital of $25,000. Former city treasurer A. S. Norton was named cashier. (Courtesy of Michael and Barbara Bigalke.)

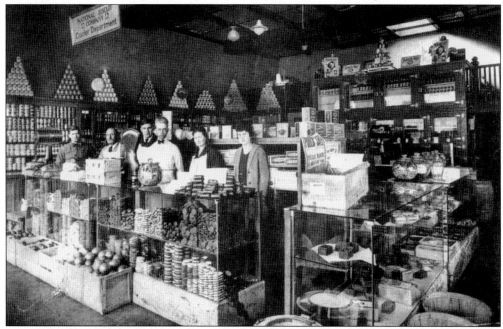

"It was during the war (W. W. II) that I went to work at the grocery store. The customer needed ration stamps, especially to buy sugar or meat. Those ration stamps had to be counted every day, posting the number of stamps with the price of the article purchased. I always had to count the stamps and deposit them at the bank, just like money, so that we could buy stock again," Martha Zickuhr Yerke Smith recounted in *Ruminations, Reflections and Expectations*. The Oberst and Wittmus Grocery is pictured. (Courtesy of Joanne Oberst Ramage.)

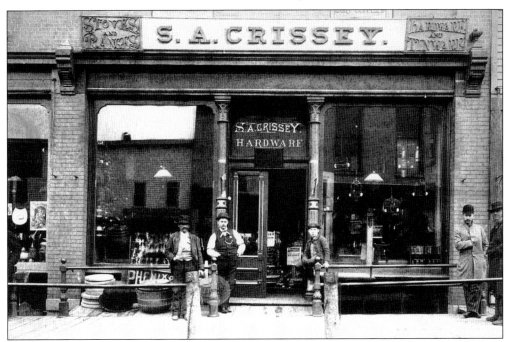

No, this photograph has not been borrowed from Galena. This was the real Marengo behind today's fake facades. Sherman A. Crissey owned this harness and hardware business, beginning in 1861. Crissey descendents are often associated with the "gingerbread home" at 553 East Grant Highway. According to the Illinois Historic Preservation Agency, a city's visible symbols of its identity should be preserved to provide its citizens a sense of security in a changing world.

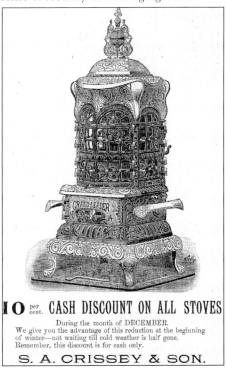

IO per cent. **CASH DISCOUNT ON ALL STOVES**

During the month of DECEMBER.
We give you the advantage of this reduction at the beginning of winter—not waiting till cold weather is half gone. Remember, this discount is for cash only.

S. A. CRISSEY & SON.

Just imagine the peacefulness of watching the soft glow of the fire spreading its illumination about the room. This stove was manufactured in Marengo at the Burgie and Collins Stove Works, and according to this December 10, 1897, advertisement, it could be purchased at S. A. Crissey and Son with a 10 percent discount.

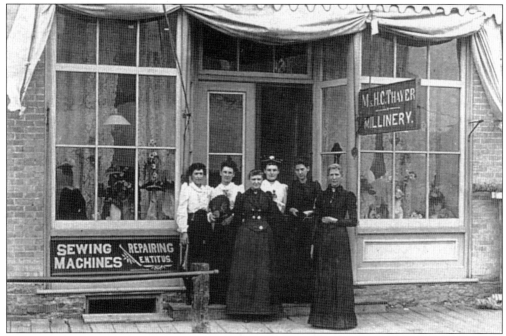

Standing closest to her millinery sign, Henrietta Axtell Thayer can be justifiably pleased with her successful business. Thayer was one of the many women in the early 20th century who successfully ran their own businesses. She was the elder sister of Emogene Axtell Robb, wife of Charles Robb. (Courtesy of Trudy Ann Robb Yates.)

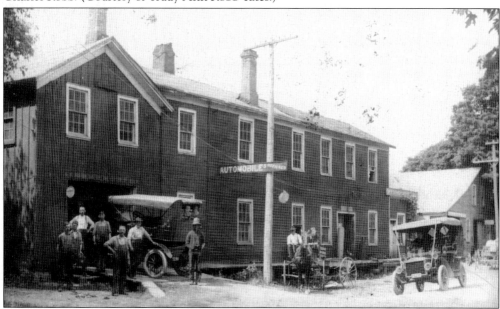

This 1909 photograph shows the old Marengo Foundry and Machine Company on West Railroad Street. Originally started by James Dietz about 1868, the business was purchased in 1872 by C. E. Kelley who increased its output capacity. The company was operated by members of the Kelley family and others for many years. In 1915, the Kelleys erected the Kelley Brothers Garage at the corner of Railroad Street and Route 23. (Courtesy of Michael and Barbara Bigalke.)

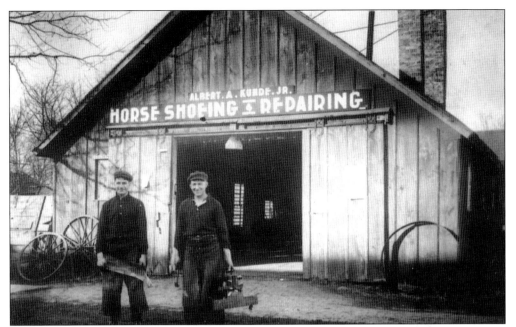

The proprietors of this most important service, the blacksmith and horseshoer, take a well-deserved break from their labors. During Marengo's first 100 years, their services, as well as those of the livery stable keepers, were in much demand and contributed greatly in maintaining Marengo's economic vitality. (Courtesy of Michael and Barbara Bigalke.)

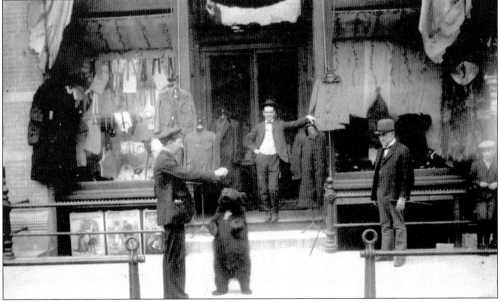

Marengo's State Street had an unusual attraction in the early 1900s. Brownie the bear was a gift to Richard Woleben, owner of the Cub Men's store. Brownie was a rascal who endeared himself, especially to the children, with his antics. He would often prance along State Street, or walk the railings that once fronted many stores along the east side of the street. He especially loved ice cream and peanuts, but could be found sitting on his haunches munching a box of Cracker Jacks.

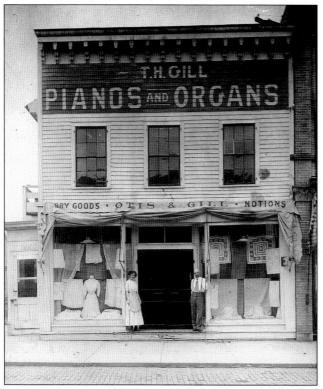

There were multiple dry goods stores operating in Marengo in the late 1800s and early 1900s. Otis and Gill operated their dry goods store at the northwest corner of West Prairie and State Streets. In 1914, Steve Otis had reached an advanced age and retired. After the closing sale, Tommy Gill continued his business in music and reopened a jewelry store at this same location.

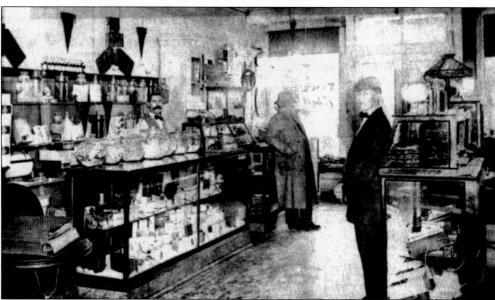

Louis Swallow's 1910 popular ice-cream parlor is pictured here. The ice-cream parlors remained the same, even into the 1940s. "And then came anxiousness that we could find a *good* parking place *on* Main [State] Street so we could watch the people! Dad would always get us a pint of Wait's ice cream and a wooden spoon. That was more fun than most kids today can imagine. There were *ALL* sorts of people on the streets!" said Dorothy Slaughter Otis in *Ruminations, Reflections and Expectations.* (Courtesy of Michael and Barbara Bigalke.)

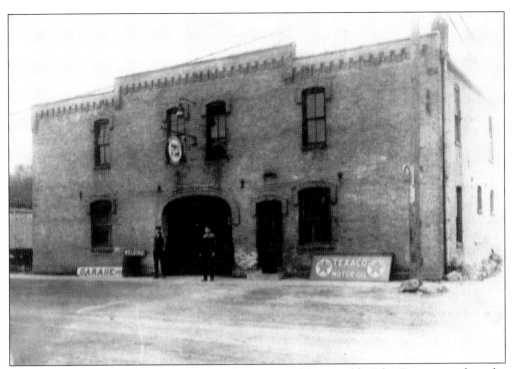

In the early 1900s, the Piper building housed a garage and livery stable. John Benton stands to the right, next to the Texaco sign. McGill Manufacturing purchased the building in 1924 and immediately initiated the renovation project. Existing in Chicago since 1878, George McGill Jr. moved their entire manufacturing plant to Marengo in 1924. "McGill was needing a plating foreman, so Dad came and applied for the job and was hired. It was quite a trip we had coming to Marengo! Dad worked at McGill thirty-five years and I'm still here," related Frank Woodruff in *Ruminations, Reflections and Expectations*. Best known for its manufacture of money changers, ticket punches, and mouse and rat traps, McGill Manufacturing enjoyed a long industrial presence. In 1943, Spencer Wernham and Norman Porter purchased McGill. (Courtesy of Barbara Koplin.)

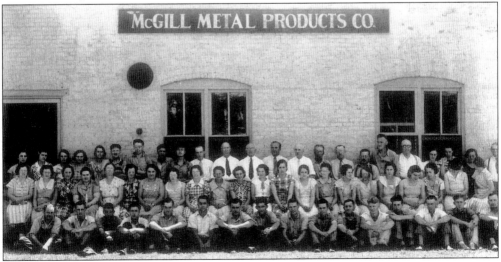

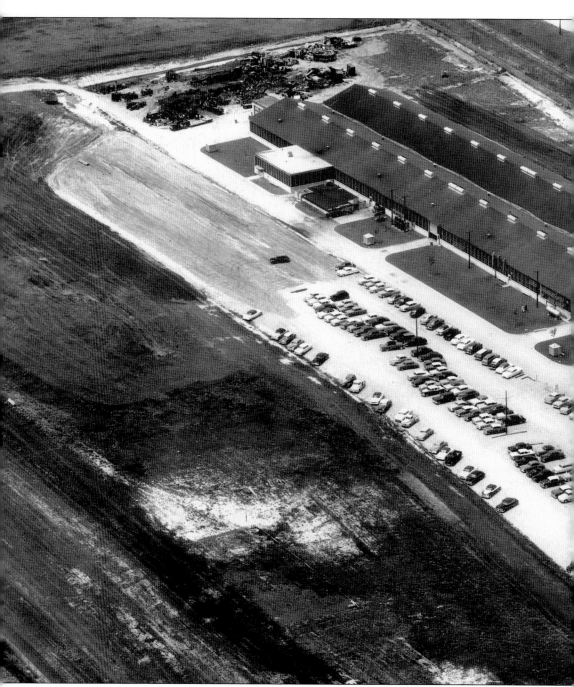

"Although the war had ended, the use of radar was increasing. Arnold Engineering got the majority of the business because of the high quality of our product and our ability to put coatings on magnets. The fibrous coating and aluminum jackets we cast on the magnets prevented tools from touching them. We made hundreds of these magnets of different designs. One remarkable thing was that Charlie Brand invented an early-type of robot which could put the heavier magnets in a die casting machine. We had the only vertical die caster in the country because it was adapted to what we were doing," said Howard Graff, according to *Ruminations, Reflections*

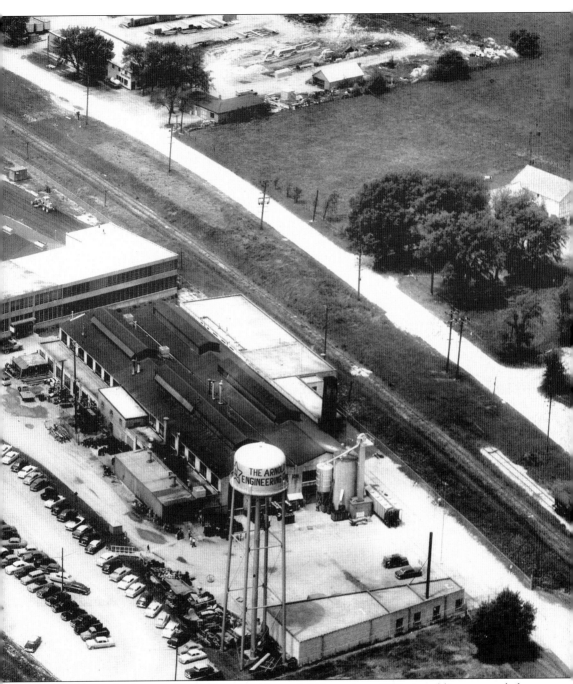

and Expectations. In the same book, Ray Arnold stated, "Along about 1943, Arnold's was awarded the Army-Navy 'E' for excellence in war production. We had quite a ceremony. About this time we had about 1,100 people working." Arnolds was also recognized for its forward thinking regarding water reclamation. In November 1964, Arnolds installed an Aerobic Digestion Sewage Treatment plant, reducing the daily need from 450,000 gallons to 50,000 gallons. (Courtesy of Charles Andrews.)

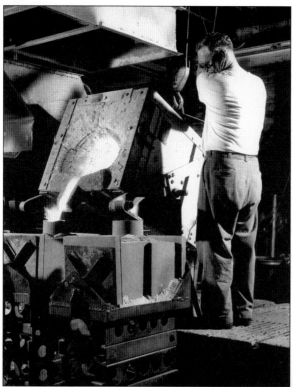

Arnold Engineering was a major manufacturer of magnetic products during World War II and thereafter. Ralph Engle started work at Arnolds in 1942, retiring in 1967. Engle worked mainly in the foundry area of the alnico department. Engle is shown pouring molten alnico from the induction furnace into a stock of sand cores. The molten alnico reached 3,000 degrees Fahrenheit. (Courtesy of Charles Andrews.)

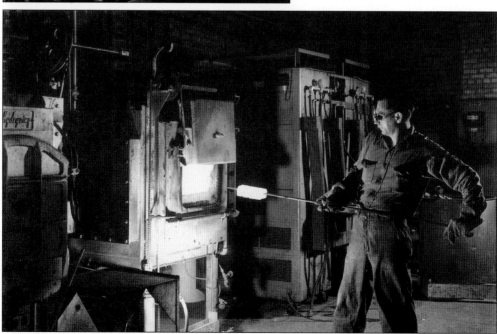

Arnold Thurow is shown taking a load of magnets from the furnace to load onto an orienting fixture. Thurow worked in the alnico heat treat department where the furnaces operated at 1,700 degrees Fahrenheit. This photograph was taken in the early 1960s. (Courtesy of Charles Andrews.)

Five

MARENGO'S FARM HERITAGE

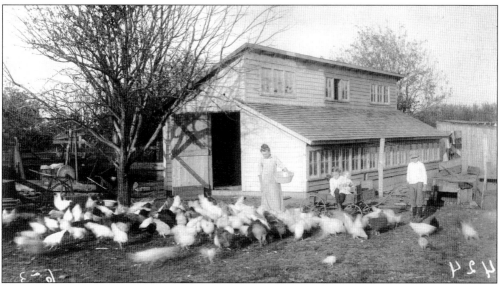

Whether it was at the Grover family farm (pictured) or the Buesing family farm, chickens were a prized possession. "It was always something to deal with those gypsies! Once mother was home alone and a group came in. She'd always heard that if you grabbed a broom and held it crossways across your chest, they'd leave. So she grabbed the broom and held it crossways! And they left! She hurried out to the chicken house and they had eighteen chickens stuffed into a bag. She barely saved them from suffocating," relates Clarence Buesing in *Ruminations, Reflections and Expectations.* In the same book, Ralph Levin is quoted as saying, "Each fall there was a big farm festival in Marengo, the event of the year. Entertainers came out from WLS (radio station), barn dance stars, some of whom are still performing (1985). The high school auditorium would be filled upstairs and down with people." (Courtesy of Glenda Jones Hughes.)

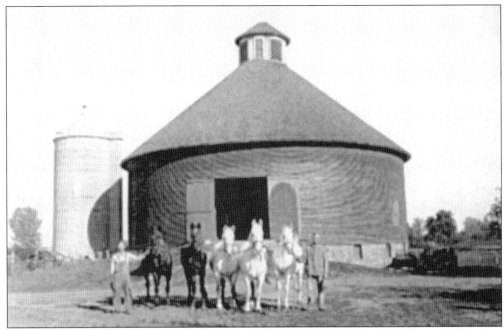

Can this barn be saved? Efforts have failed so far. It is still standing in 2007 but in a declining condition. It has been deemed restorable by a barn specialist. Since the cupola blew off in a storm, the interior is open to the elements. It is the last standing round barn in McHenry County. Built on River Road in 1897 by the Willard brothers, it is an example of engineering expertise and precise craftsmanship. (Courtesy of Elmer Nelson family.)

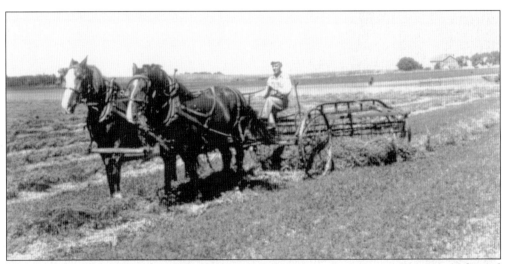

"That summer [1936] brought a plague of chinch bugs because it was so dry. Harold [Yerke] remembers how the bundles of silage filler would be filled with them. He explained that the bundles were cut by a binder and dropped on the ground. The men would then walk along behind with a fork and pitch the bundles up onto a hay wagon," said Abe Dunker in *Ruminations, Reflections and Expectations*. (Courtesy of Frank J. Mack family.)

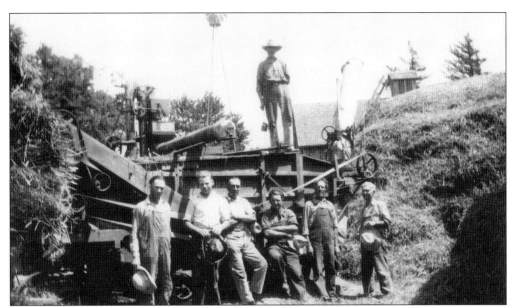

Threshing was one job where many hands were needed. Men and women joined forces to get the job done and provide a hot meal. The threshing crew is at the Willard Hartman farm, Hartman Road, in Riley Township. All are unidentified except Millard Hartman (on left) and August Hartman (second from right). The unidentified are most likely nearby neighbors. "While the men were out in the fields, the women would be working away in the kitchen. It was unbelievable the meals that could be made on just an old cook stove. It has often been debated as to who worked harder on these occasions, the men or the women!" Abe Dunker related in *Ruminations, Reflections and Expectations*. (Courtesy of Robert Hartman.)

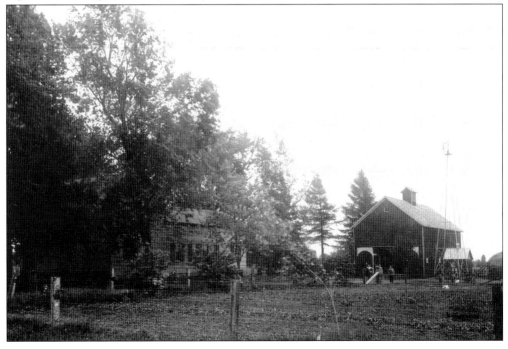

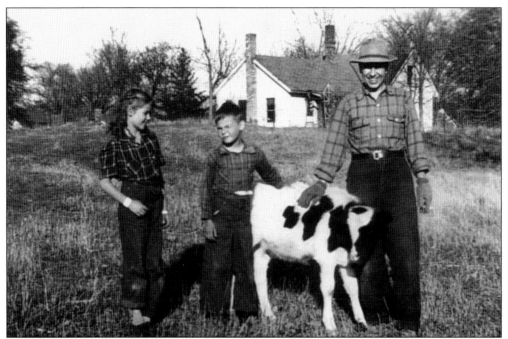

It was not too unusual for Marengo's early residents to keep a cow, chickens, or horses "in town," especially if they lived on streets abutting farm land. Seventy-five years ago, streets like Dietz, Maple, Grant Highway, State, and even the far ends of Prairie, all qualified. Allison and John Pringle had the best of two worlds, city comforts and the neighbor's calf. (Courtesy of Allison Pringle Seaton.)

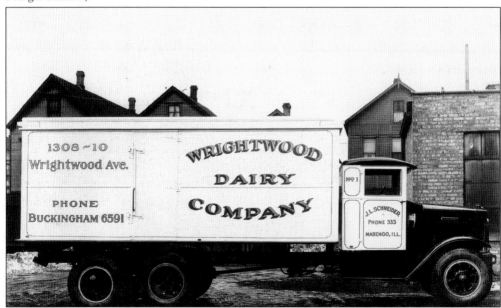

The address on the truck box is clearly not in Marengo. But notice the name, phone, and address on the truck cab. The truck belonged to J. L. Schneider, Marengo, Illinois, taking the name of Marengo to wherever he hauled his Wrightwood Dairy products. His deliveries were probably in the Chicago suburbs. (Courtesy of Karen Hartman.)

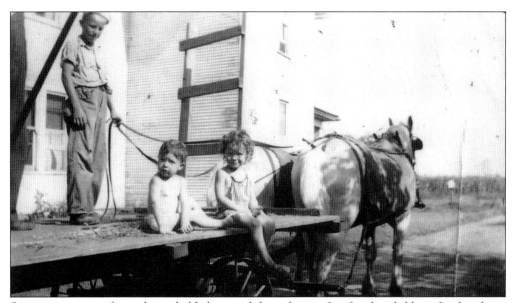

Summertime on a farm always held the possibility of extra fun for the children. In the above 1938 photograph, one can almost feel the July sun bearing down on human and animal alike. On the Deneen farm in Marengo Township, Patricia and Mary Jane Deneen are getting a ride under the watchful eye of Albert Hufford. (Courtesy of Mary Jane Deneen Bauman.)

Kathryn Deneen closely watches as young Tom Deneen tries his hand at putting gas in the tank of this Minneapolis Moline U. Olin Averrill does not seem too concerned! "Tractors had come in the 20's but we still used the horses for things like corn planting and dragging. By the mid 30's most everyone was using tractors for plowing and disking. Hybrid seed corn came in about then too," said Emil Olbrich in *Ruminations, Reflections and Expectations*. (Courtesy of Mary Jane Deneen Bauman.)

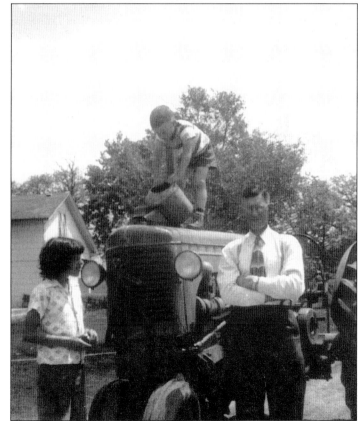

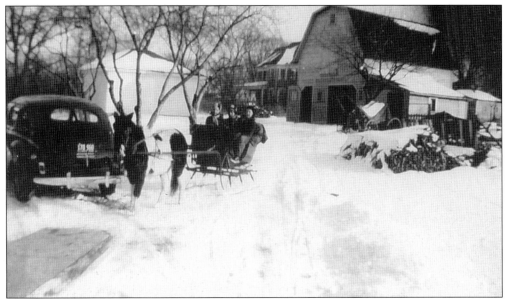

This is a photograph of the Henry Nulle farmette at 423 West Grant. "The milk truck from town could make it this far [Route 23 and Anthony Road]. The center of our yard would be two deep with [our neighbor's] milk cans! Farmers used their 'stoneboats' to get their milk this far. The back door was always open, and Gram would have a coffee pot on the stove for their neighbors," recalls Don Anthony, according to *Ruminations, Reflections and Expectations*. (Courtesy of Alice Nulle.)

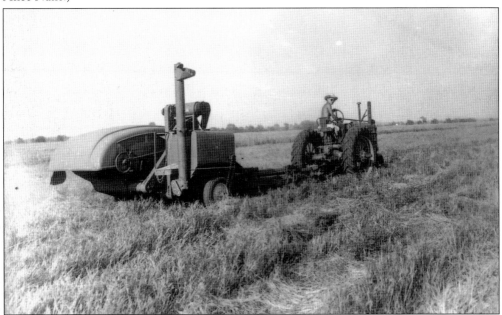

The farming industry has been central to the prosperity of Marengo since its beginning. So it was important to have local sources of farm machinery. In the early 20th century, E. S. Cadwell was one of Marengo's largest, most popular, and best-known dealers. His line of equipment ranged from rakes to threshing machines. He also dealt in Staver and Abbott as well as Henney Buggy company carriages. (Courtesy of Frank J. Mack family.)

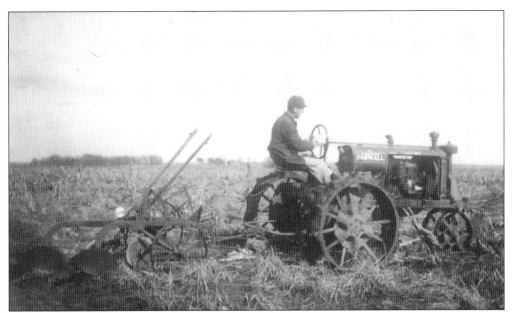

This unidentified farmer was contributing to the significant local farming industry. The Marengo-area farmers were well represented in the early 1900s by businessman M. Zimplemann, who was president of the McHenry County Agricultural Society and representative to the Eighth Congressional District of the Illinois State Agricultural Society. (Courtesy of Frank J. Mack family.)

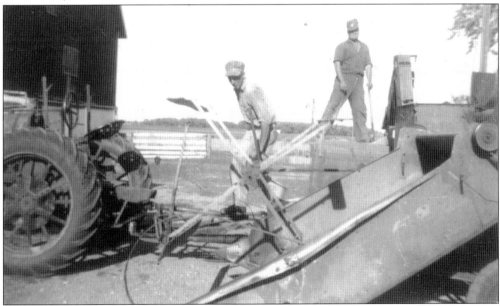

Adin Slaughter (left) and Bob Eicksteadt are shown in this early-1940s photograph. In *Ruminations, Reflections and Expectations*, Slaughter recalls that "The worst time we ever had exchanging help was during World War II when we were encouraged by the government to raise hemp for rope. George [Eicksteadt] didn't like it and neither did Rudy [Mueller] or I. You *couldn't* pitch those bundles up on a wagon very easily, they were so heavy! Loading them for delivery to Kirkland was something else again!"

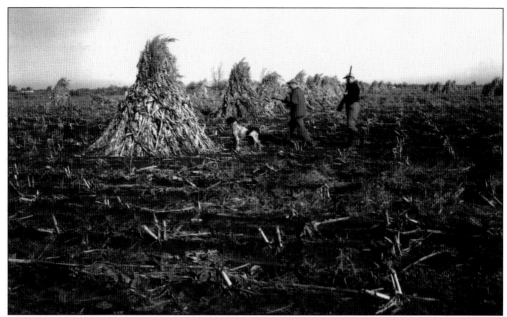

Farmers did not work all the time! Fall usually signaled the time when the crops were harvested and under cover for winter feeding. The farmers pictured had to deal with those corn shocks but still had time for pheasant hunting. (Courtesy of Frank J. Mack family.)

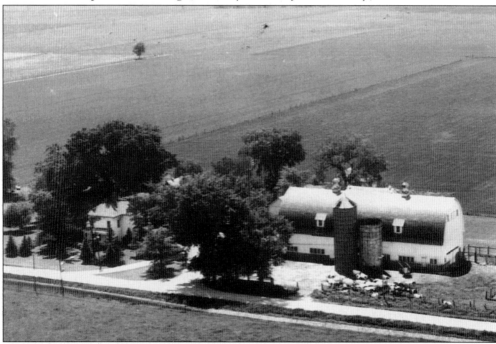

This 1940s aerial photograph is of the Fred J. Miller dairy farm, located on Miller Road in Marengo Township. "Many of the organizations or areas of social gatherings for farmers 30 or 40 years ago [1945–1955] have disappeared. The Grange was the farmers' main social organization. Along with the lectures and farm-related study, we'd have potlucks, singing and sometimes card playing," Mabel McKee Ratcliff remembered in *Ruminations, Reflections and Expectations.*

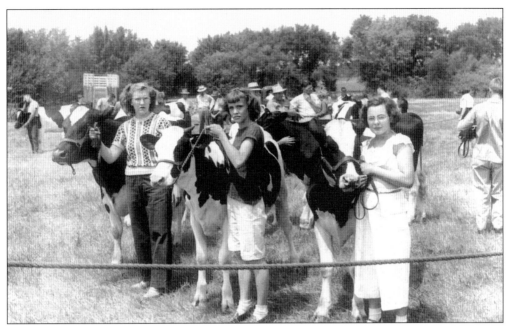

Wilda Nevel (left) and Dorothy Slaughter (center) came away with first and second place in the annual Black and White Showmanship Show in 1951–1952. They both were members of the Riley Ramblers 4-H Club. The girl on the right is from Hebron, Illinois.

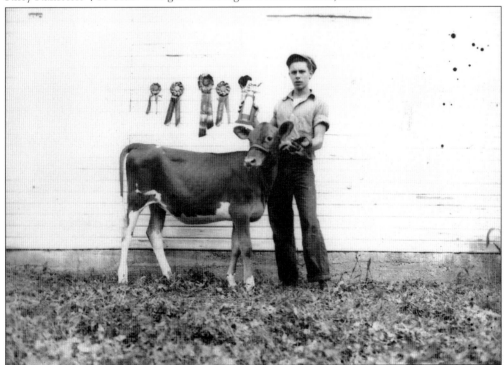

In 1949, Future Farmers of America (FFA) member Larry West came home with championship ribbons for his Guernsey yearling heifer. The West family farmed and lived in Riley Township. (Courtesy of Frank J. Mack family.)

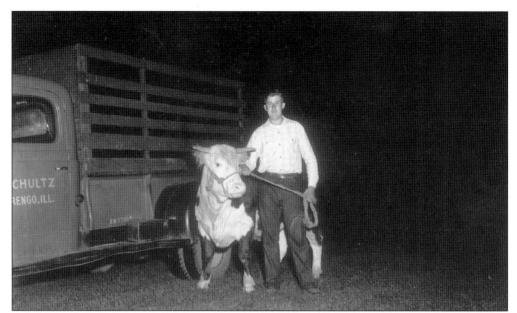

A farm products show was started by the Kiwanis Club and businessmen in 1927. This show allowed the farmers to show their produce and receive prizes for their fruits, vegetables, livestock, and other products. The show continued for many years and was extremely popular. As many as 1,300 persons regularly attended the shows, which were held at the community high school. Awards were contributed by the businessmen who also sponsored the entertainment. (Courtesy of Frank J. Mack family.)

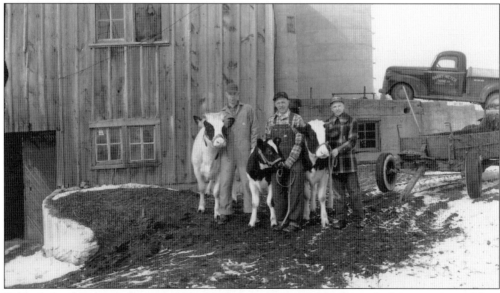

"I liked the dairy cow. Every farm had a dairy on it but it slowly worked into grain and hog country. McHenry County was one of the top milk producing counties in Illinois. I think it would be good for the world, yet, if they'd put about 20 million farm families back on the land instead of having three guys do it all," said Dr. George Buehler in *Ruminations, Reflections and Expectations*. Pictured here from left to right are Dale, Harry, and Don Meyer on their Riley Township farm. (Courtesy of Frank J. Mack family.)

Six

READING, WRITING, AND RELIGION

Built of Dundee brick, the five-story Marengo Collegiate Institute was built in 1856–1957 on five acres, for a cost of $20,000. Accommodating 150 students, the institute was located on Sponable Hill, at the west end of West Prairie Street. It formally opened on September 30, 1857.

Two hundred dollars provided 16 years tuition. The institute was under the care of the Presbytery of Chicago. Funds became a problem almost immediately. Just four months after opening, the board of trustees closed the building. On March 6, 1858, Dr. Charles C. Miller opened a school in the basement of the Presbyterian Church for 30–40 former students of the institute.

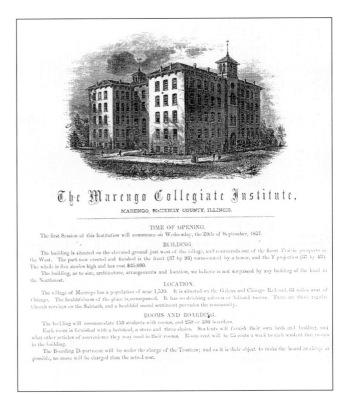

The Marengo Collegiate Institute.

MARENGO, McHENRY COUNTY, ILLINOIS.

TIME OF OPENING.

The first Session of this Institution will commence on Wednesday, the 30th of September, 1857.

BUILDING.

The building is situated on the elevated ground just west of the village, and commands one of the finest Prairie prospects in the West. The part now erected and finished in the front (37 by 93) surmounted by a tower, and the T projection (37 by 43). The whole is five stories high and has cost $25,000.

The building, as to size, architecture, arrangements and location, we believe is not surpassed by any building of the kind in the Northwest.

LOCATION.

The village of Marengo has a population of near 1,500. It is situated on the Galena and Chicago Railroad, 65 miles west of Chicago. The healthfulness of the place is unsurpassed. It has no drinking saloons or billiard rooms. There are three regular Church services on the Sabbath, and a healthful moral sentiment pervades the community.

ROOMS AND BOARDING.

The building will accommodate 150 students with rooms, and 250 or 300 boarders.

Each room is furnished with a bedstead, a stove and three chairs. Students will furnish their own beds and bedding, and what other articles of convenience they may need in their rooms. Room rent will be 25 cents a week to each student that rooms in the building.

The Boarding Department will be under the charge of the Trustees; and as it is their object to make the board as cheap as possible, no more will be charged than the actual cost.

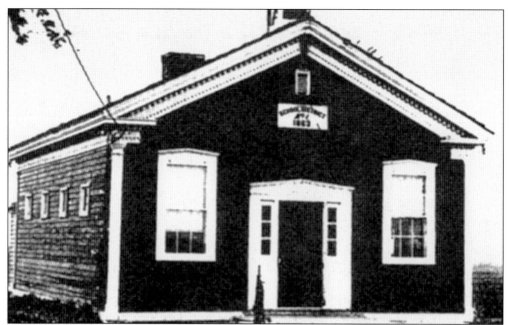

Seen here is South Riley School. "So many of these one-room schools have been converted to homes or just left to deteriorate. But it's always made me happy to drive by South Riley [School]. Dr. Ovitz keeps it is so beautifully 'original.' I went to South Riley School. Sometimes there would be 26 kids! We kids only had to walk a mile to school. My teachers were Thelma Yerke Spaulding, Vera Wilde, Tillie Foster and Hilda Benson," recalls Jeanette Mackey Walters in *Ruminations, Reflections and Expectations*. (Courtesy of McHenry County Historical Society.)

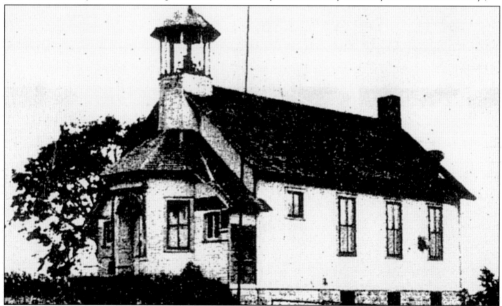

On October 2, 1994, the McHenry County Historical Society confirmed the historical integrity of the former one-room Diggins School on east River Road. Attending the historical plaque placing celebration were former students Marcella Wright Spears, Harold Wright, Carl Bockman, Frances Conley, Bud Standish, Joe Baronak, and teacher Evelyn Johansen.

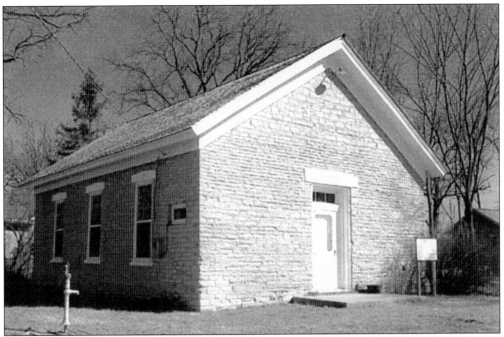

The Pringle School was built in 1867 of limestone quarried from the Galena Road (Grant Highway) quarry. Land was donated by Patterson and Isabella McDonald Pringle, on whose farm the land was located. Patterson and Isabella settled on River Road in 1849. Many Pringle-Wilson relatives taught at the Pringle School. This was the third, and best, schoolhouse to be built in this area of River Road since the first settler, John Beldin, arrived in 1835.

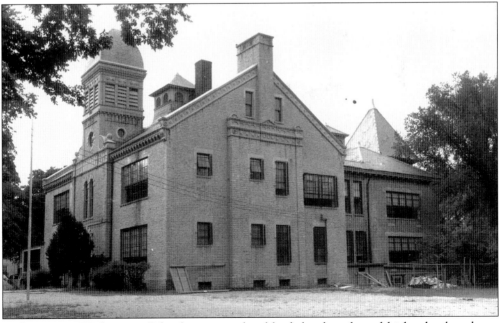

Built in 1883, Washington School accommodated both local grade and high school students. Shown here is the grade school portion, which faced West Grant Highway. Classrooms were located on all three levels of the building.

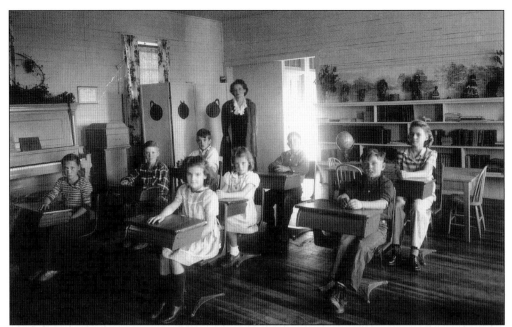

As evidenced by this 1944 picture, the students of Esther Robb, in the Riley Township Eicksteadt School, were surrounded with learning opportunities. "Social studies and literature lessons took on a special meaning with Mrs. Robb. Recess time was often a continuation of learning as she encouraged and instructed the older students in the building of Indian teepees, totem poles and igloos. We'd all have a hand in creating the wall mural above the book cases," said Dorothy Slaughter Otis, according to *Ruminations, Reflections and Expectations*.

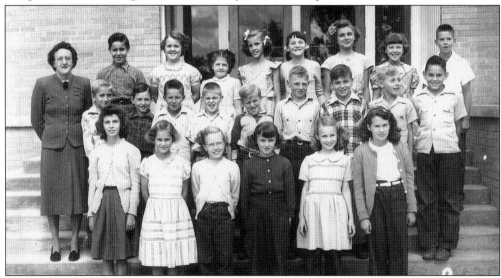

Pictured are the first fifth- and sixth-grade classes in the new District 18 school building. They are, from left to right, (first row) Beverly Kolberg, Darlene Krause, Myrna Joyce Crawford, Betty Eshbaugh, Rose Mary West, and Marlene Ulrich; (second row) Lester Leuck, Kenny Meyer, Leonard Pfaffinger, Charles Grossen, Darwin Eshbaugh, Bill Markison, Ernie Martz Jr., Ron McKee, and Gene Krause; (third row) Eleanor Huber, Bill Ardell, Kay Dolder, Bonnie Schuring, Dorothy Slaughter, Crystal Kearney, Shirley Fidder, Jean Pineger, and Dick Burnside.

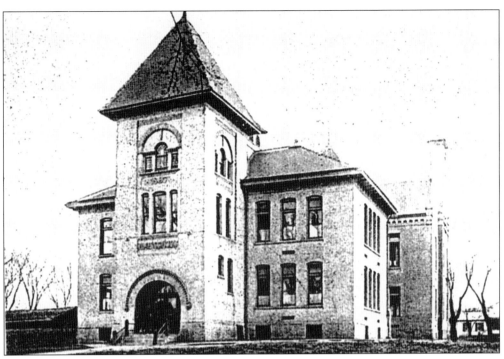

Washington School was built in 1883 and, until 1925, was occupied jointly by the grade and high school students. Shown above is the high school portion, which faced Washington Street, while the grade school portion faced Grant Highway. The newly-constructed community high school, on East Grant Highway, opened in 1925. In 1928, the Washington School was completely remodeled for the exclusive use by the grade school students. Sadly, the community lost this grand structure to the wrecking ball in 1993, replaced by a McDonald's fast-food restaurant. "Ray's Chicago relatives would come out [to Marengo] and say, 'why do you send your [5] kids to school in a little town like this?' Our kids never had any trouble when they went on to college. They did a lot better than many of the city kids," said Wilmet Arnold, speaking about husband Ray Arnold, in *Ruminations, Reflections and Expectations*. (Courtesy of Michael and Barbara Bigalke.)

"Haste Not, Rest Not."

—※ THIRTEENTH ※ ANNUAL ※—

Commencement Exercises

OF THE

Marengo High School

OPERA HOUSE,

Thursday evening, June 6th,

MDCCCLXXXIX.

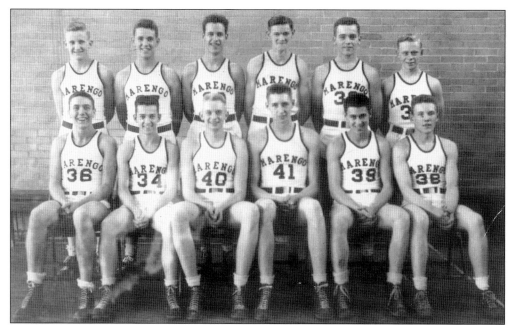

Marengo Community High School's 1946 basketball team includes, from left to right, (first row) Robert Basely, Ken Steig, Bill Shearer, Elmer Behnke (later the coach at Bradley University), Earl Hahn, and Lyle Miller; (second row) Ed Carney, Herb Simpson, Elmer Rudy, Harris Penney, Macy Holiday, and Gerald O'Cock. (Courtesy of Shirley Pinnow Kitchen.)

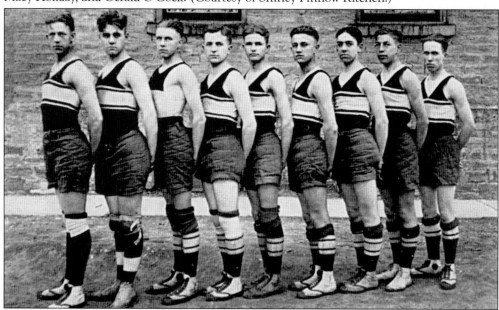

The high school had organized a basketball team in 1919. Games were played in the community hall, created by E. D. Patrick, on the upper floor of the First National Bank. Some of the opponents were Belvidere, Woodstock, Harvard, and Huntley. Members of the team include (not in order) Lloyd Taylor, Maurice Kitchen, Stanley Woleben, Clifford Kitchen, Joseph Patterson, Howard Tanner, Morel Miller, Dell Coon, William Church, and Herbert Kutzner. (Courtesy of Shirley Pinnow Kitchen.)

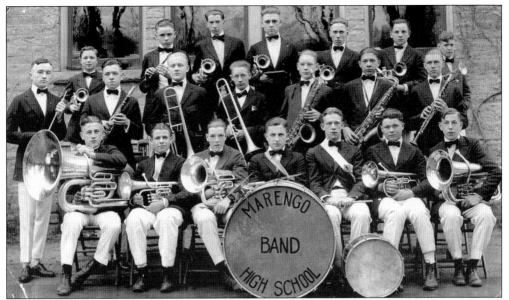

Mr. Sebastian was asked to organize a high school band at the beginning of the 1919 school year. He actively solicited all interested students, with only four boys responding. But soon others joined. They were thoroughly drilled in the marching form. Their jackets were dark blue with white trousers. (Courtesy of Shirley Pinnow Kitchen.)

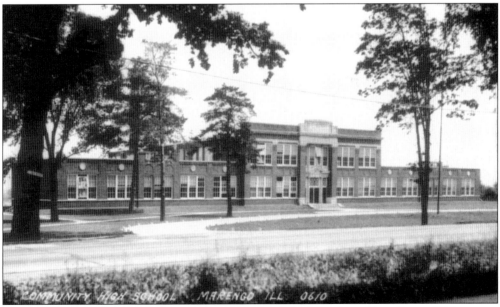

Classes began in the new Marengo Community High School on East Grant Highway on December 2, 1925. The first District 154 Board of Education was composed of president J. H. Patterson and secretary O. C. Wright with members F. B. Johnson, Neill C. Dunham, and P. W. Andrews. Prior to creating District 154, Marengo and Union each had separate high schools. The first class to graduate from Marengo's high school was in 1875, with six members. Those members were Frank Hastings, Edwin Treat, Alice Wells, Morell Webb, Addie Gochey, and Charles Seward. (Courtesy of Marengo Public Library.)

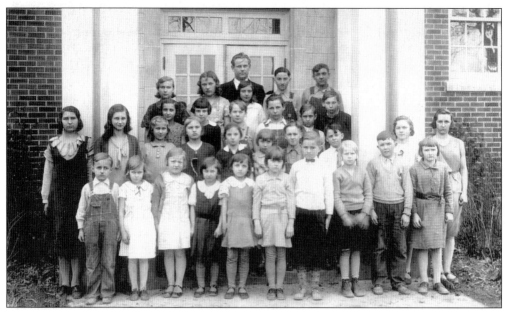

The Harmony School class of 1933 includes, from left to right, (first row) Duane Diedrich, Ella Daulby, Lois Meinke, unidentified, unidentified, Marjorie Church, Loyal Humbrecht, Dorothy Wacin, Russell Imhoff, and LaVerne Imhoff; (second row) Ella Harting, Elfrieda Schmuck, Stella Avelas, Ella Henning, Margaret Getty, Norma Wilkens, Frederich Diedrich, unidentified, Elvira Meinke, and Flora Imhoff; (third row) Gertrude Schmuck, unidentified, James Wacin, Bill Wacin, Harvey Laue, and Ernie Harting; (fourth row) Francis Henning, Evelyn Rambo, Eleanor Laue, Harold Getty, and Floyd Laue. (Courtesy of Eleanor Laue Phelps.)

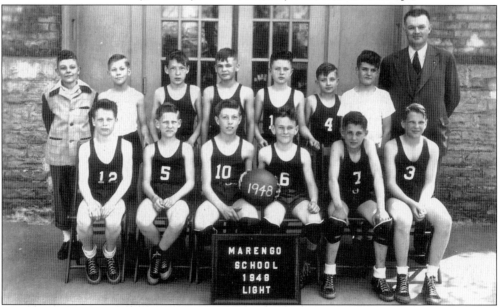

This Marengo Grade School basketball squad is made up of, from left to right, (first row) Bruce Davis, Dell Coon, John Kitchen, unidentified, Ross Kitchen, and Robert Piskie; (second row) Tom Driver, Gerald Swafford, James Hegberg, John Pringle, John Ratcliff, Frank Gray, David Graff, and coach Kenneth Wilson. (Courtesy of Shirley Pinnow Kitchen.)

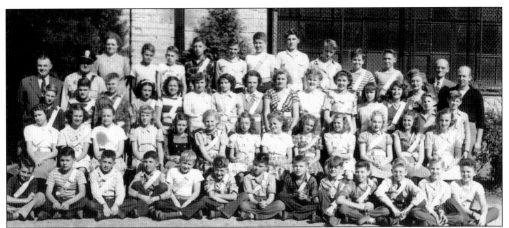

Washington School had a large patrol squad in 1946–1947. They are, from left to right, (first row) Franklin Gray, Lt. Stephen Otis, Ross Kitchen, Harry Wolf, Charles Kunde Jr., Lt. David Olinger, Jr. Capt. Joseph Havens, Robert Schmars, Robert Foster, Francis Havens, Edward Winter, Gerald Swofford, and John Ratcliff; (second row) Alice Lockhart, Joan Driver, Barbara Stone, Sandra Willis, Sandra Wolf, Jeanne Otis, Janet Schneider, Jeanette Mack, Joan Mack, Sally Thomas, Carolyn Fry, Lt. Delores Anthony, and Sally Shenberger; (third row) Frederick Kakac, David Graff, Rozel Corson, Nancy Wilcox, Sandra Helper, Lt. Barbara Weaver, Donna Carter, Sandra Kelley, Joan Cates, Delores Westfall, Carole Courier, Dorothy Stokes, Mary Kubly, Lt. John Repp, and Capt. Donald McMackin; (fourth row) Kenneth Wilson (principal), sponsor Chief Joseph Lapinski, Violet Strawn, John Pringle, Jack Dickerson, John Kitchen, Robert Piske, William Griebel, Charles Ackman, Roy Hanson, Thomas Feirtag, James Hegberg, Gladys Wilson, cosponsor E. H. Stassen (Chicago Motor Club), and cosponsor John Fisher (Veterans of Foreign Wars). (Courtesy of Michael and Barbara Bigalke.)

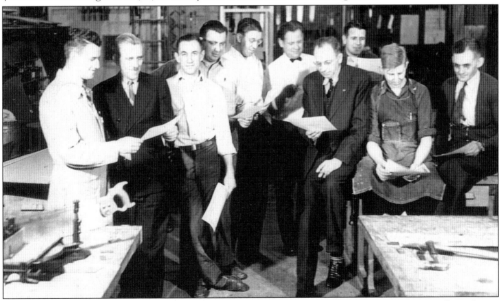

Adult evening classes were held at the high school during the 1940s–1950s for interested residents. Kenneth Walthers led the building classes. Pictured from left to right are Kenneth Walthers, Rev. William Ellis Lampson, Clifford Kitchen, unidentified, Norman Piskie, unidentified, Arlie Shearer, Don Pringle, unidentified, and unidentified. (Courtesy of Marilyn Walthers Stone.)

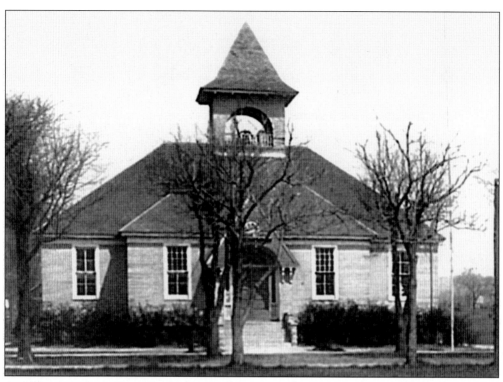

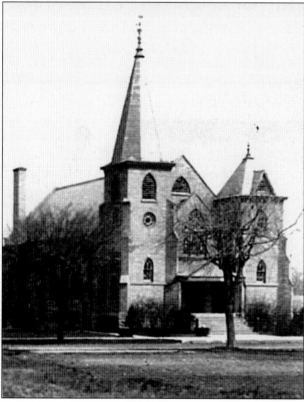

Zion Lutheran School was established in 1888. At the encouragement of regular teacher H. E. Krentz and Pastor Paul Doederlein, a new, modern school was erected in 1904. Following the death in 1906 of Krentz, J. W. Feirtag was hired. He taught until 1924. The goal to have the school accredited with the high school occurred in 1913, when the four eighth-grade pupils, Amanda Zickuhr, Alma Cassier, Fred Dunker, and Erhardt Hinz, easily passed the examinations.

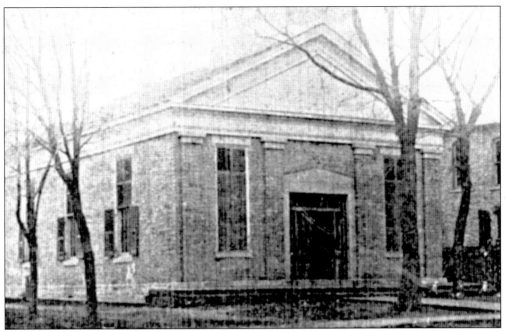

The Methodist Episcopal church was the first church to actually organize. This was in 1837. Construction was begun on the above church in 1855. Several other Methodist churches, including Free Methodist and Wesleyan, organized, but disbanded after a few years. The present day Methodist church, at the corner of Taylor and Washington Streets, was built and dedicated in 1897.

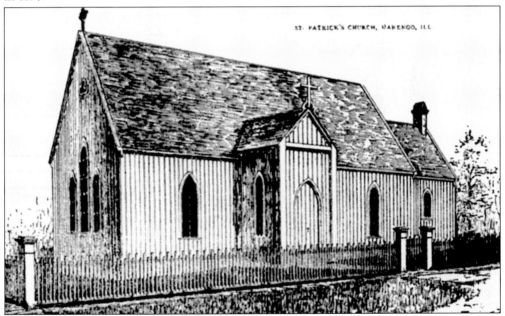

Although the Catholic church did not become established for many years, in 1837, a Catholic missionary post was established in Hartland for everyone in the area. The above Episcopal church was sold to the Catholics in 1864. By 1907, the Sacred Heart parish had been gathering strength and membership, resulting in the building of the present-day brick church.

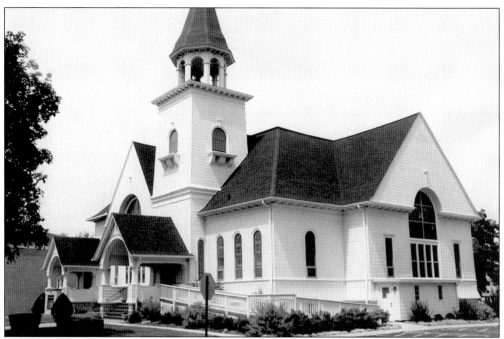

The first church services were held in Calvin Spencer's cabin. In December 1840, the Pleasant Grove Baptist Church was organized. Since they were then meeting in a frame building in Coral, the name was changed in 1851 to the Coral Baptist Church. As Marengo grew, the members felt it important to also have a church in the village. This new building served the congregation until 1897, when the current church (above) was built.

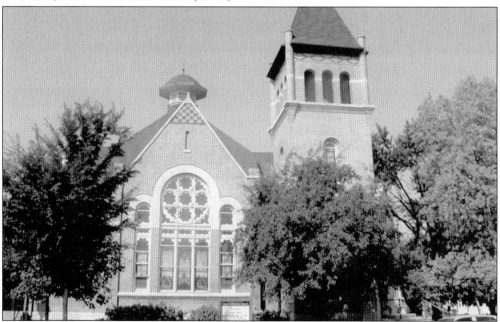

A group of the faithful met to discuss the organization of a church. Representatives of the Presbytery of Wisconsin acted as the organizing committee. The building of a meetinghouse was begun and completed in June 1852. The above Presbyterian church was built in 1899.

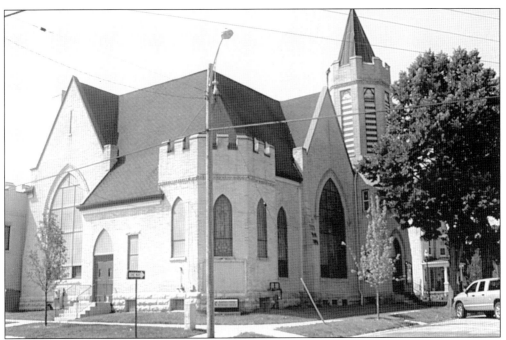

An early 1900s copy of the *Journal of Fine Arts* says, "There are six denominations maintaining regular services, three having churches among the finest in the state." These words of acknowledgement, written over 100 years ago, are easy to appreciate. The current Methodist church (above) was built 1897.

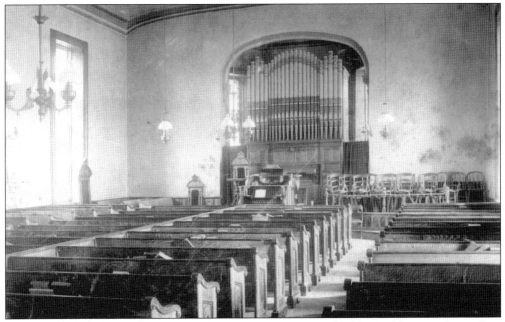

This postcard shows the interior of the early Methodist church. The building was located on East Washington Street, facing the street, where there currently is a parking lot. After the church members built their new church in 1897, this building was used for many years as a movie theater. (Courtesy of Michael and Barbara Bigalke.)

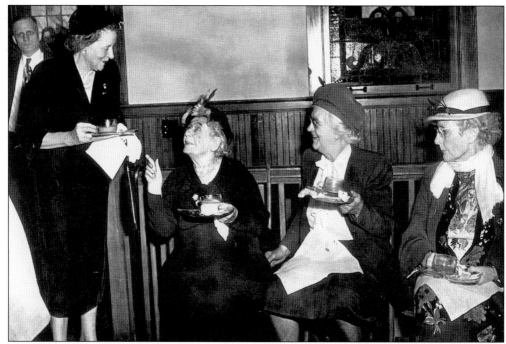

Four of Marengo's great ladies enjoy their refreshments at the Presbyterian church. This photograph was taken about 1950. All were lifelong residents. From left to right are Esther Robb, Carolyn Coon, Jane Stanford, and Billie Woodard. Robb was a teacher and organized the centennial pageant, Coon was an early business woman and longtime musician, and Stanford was associated with education her entire life. (Courtesy of Trudy Ann Robb Yates.)

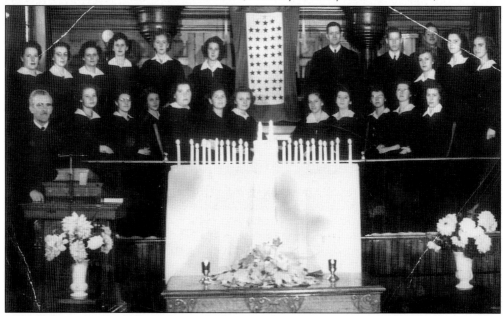

This photograph was taken in the Methodist church in the 1940s when William Ellis Lampson was pastor. Based on the flag and lit candles, it appears to be a special prayer service for the men and women serving in World War II. (Courtesy of Shirley Pinnow Kitchen.)

Seven

CIVIC AND SOCIAL

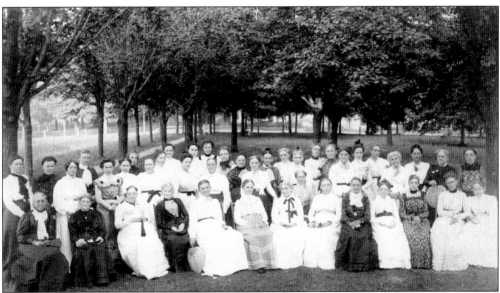

In recognition of and love for her dear friends who were members of the Ladies Home Circle, radio celebrity "Aunt Em," or Emma VanAlstyne Lanning, wrote "The Home Circle," a poem dedicated to the Home Circle of Marengo, Illinois. "Sitting tonight in the twilight glow / As the drifting shadows come and go / My thoughts go back to the old home place / And again I see each dear, loved face / . . . Those friends of yore, friends tried, true / No others can fill their place with you / It matter not how far you may roam / Our thoughts all turn to the friends at home / . . . The dear Home Circle comes to my mind / It's members always so true, so kind / Some here, some there, some have passed along / Across the River they sing the song. . . . When we too pass to that other shore / Where sorrow and parting is known no more / We will meet, and take them by the hand / The ones we loved in our Home Circle band." (Courtesy of Michael and Barbara Bigalke.)

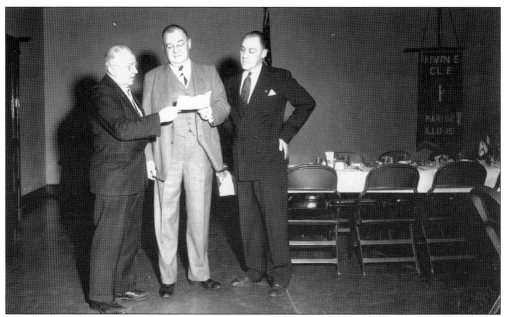

Ken Cooper was very involved with the local Kiwanis Club for many years. He is shown on the right, probably during a presentation of funds to the representatives of the regional or national organization. Cooper was the owner of the Cooper Funeral Home for many years. (Courtesy of Frank J. Mack family.)

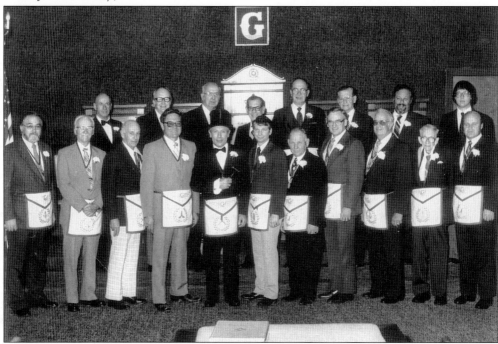

Officially organized October 5, 1853, the Masonic Lodge, No. 138, Ancient Free and Accepted Masons, remains an active organization in 2007. William Dougherty and C. B. Whittemore had built a large addition to their blocks especially for the use of the Marengo Lodge, Lansing Chapter and the Order of the Eastern Star. This home was dedicated on May 6, 1913.

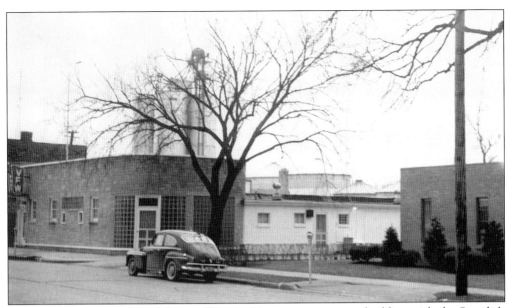

In the 1940s, the Veterans of Foreign Wars building was a one-story building with the Standish Grain Elevators located behind it and the McGills office building to the right. Because of its popularity, a second floor was added where daily meals could be served by the auxiliary and more dances could be held. As finances dwindled, the building was sold to the city and dedicated as the new city hall on August 11, 1978. (Courtesy of Michael and Barbara Bigalke.)

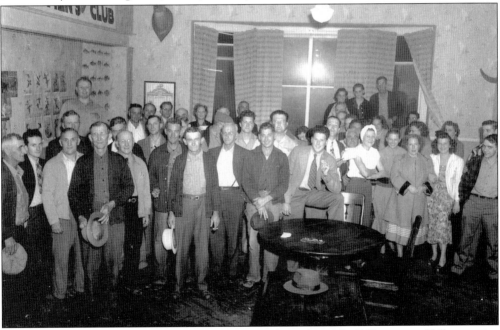

Unfortunately, the editors do not have information about this early 1950s group of folks meeting in the Marengo Sportsmen's Club. But because of the number of people in attendance, it appears to have been a successful organization. The third person from the right in the first row appears to be an Anthony. Please contact the Marengo Society for Historic Preservation with information about this group. (Courtesy Frank J. Mack family.)

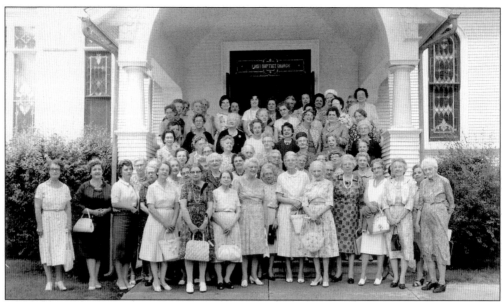

In March 1878, the wives of the Farmer's Club members decided to organize an auxiliary called the Ladies Home Circle. Charter members were Mesdames E. H. Seward, William Boise, M. B. Metcalf, R. M. Patrick, L. W. Sheldon, Alfred Patrick, Frank Hackley, ? Bruce, Lester Barber, Rush Bartholomew, Sherman Bartholomew, A. R. Parkhurst, Chapin Wilcox, ? Owen, Joel Smith, Robert Smith, and ? Bingham. This group is still active in 2007. This picture was taken at their centennial meeting held at the First Baptist church.

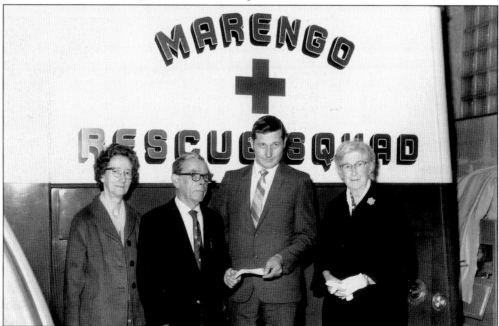

Don Zichuhr, representative of the Marengo Rescue Squad, is shown accepting a financial donation from Ann Peterson (left), A. Bazzar, and Ida Rowland. At that time, the rescue squad was not a local taxing body but was totally supported by community and individual donations. (Courtesy of Gordon Lee.)

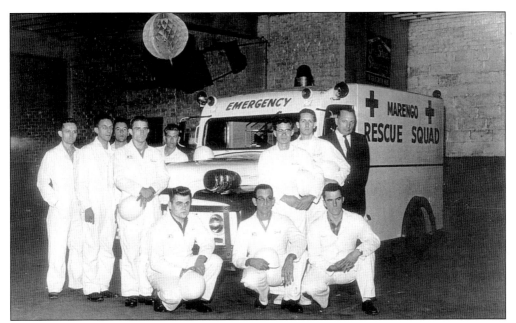

At the recommendation of the Jaycee's rescue squad committee, information-gathering meetings were held with members of the Walworth, Wisconsin, and Harvard, Illinois, squads. Shown are the early members of the Marengo Rescue Squad, from left to right, (first row) John Lockhart, Tony Mack, and Ronald Davis; (second row) Paul Bowers, Dave Nelson, Bill Shielbergen, Gordon Lee, Noel Lambert, Dennis Madaus, Denzel Thompson, and unidentified. Many of these members were employed at Arnold Engineering. (Courtesy of Gordon Lee.)

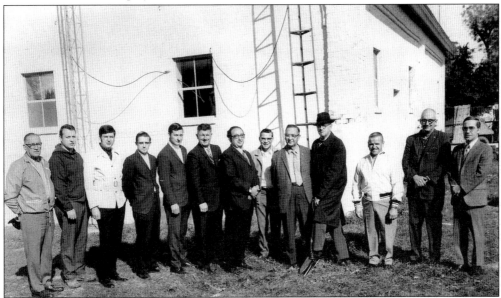

Ground was broken in 1971 for an addition to the public works building, which would also accommodate the rescue squad vehicles. Shown from left to right are Clifford Kitchen, unidentified, Robert Kolberg, Gordon Lee, Gary Zichuhr, alderman Don Hubbs, alderman Ralph Levin, Denny Madaus, Otis Cripe, Mayor Herman Buesing, aldermen Lee Soucie, Adin Slaughter, and Raymond Clemens. (Courtesy of Michael and Barbara Bigalke.)

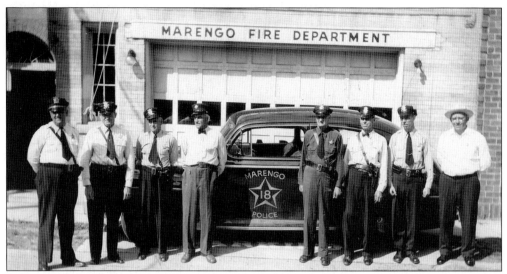

Full- and part-time policemen pose in front of the old city hall/fire department in 1935. At that time, the department was run by several full-time officers and part-timers who helped with traffic control for special events. Pictured from left to right are Chief Fred Nelson, unidentified, Harold Hyde, William Piskie Sr., Monty George, John Benton, and two unidentified. (Courtesy of Frank J. Mack family.)

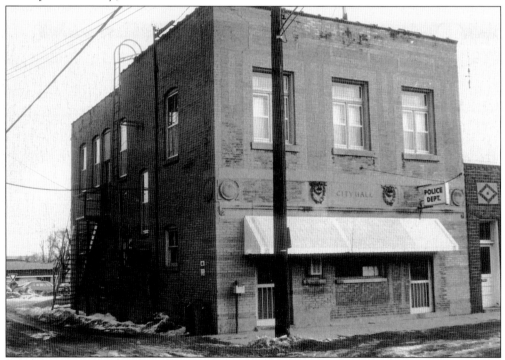

Built in 1909 for $5,054.28, the city hall was a source of community pride. The basement contained the steam heating plant, while the main floor housed the fire department and the three-cage jail in the back. Additional cages could be added. A toilet room was located in this area. The second floor held the police magistrate's office and the council chambers, which was large enough to hold 150 persons. (Courtesy of Michael and Barbara Bigalke.)

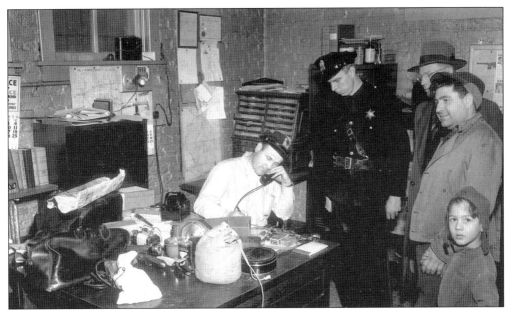

The reasons for this police station gathering is unknown. Has stolen property been recovered? By the looks of the items lying on the desk, it may be a possibility. Officer Curley VanDerValk is on the telephone, the other officer is unidentified. Standing next is high school superintendant Everett C. Nichols and Bobby Carroccia with his son John. (Courtesy of Frank J. Mack family.)

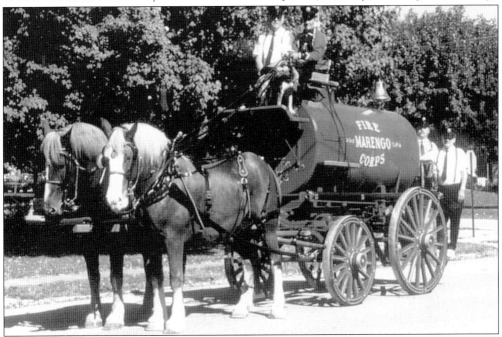

Fireman Martin Gallagher, with the help of many other firemen, restored this old Marengo Fire Corp Studebacker water tanker. Built in Dixon for the city of Marengo to use in watering down dirt streets, it was eventually given to the fire corp. The Olbrich farms purchased it for hauling whey. After sitting unused for many years, it was given to the Marengo Fire Protection District. (Courtesy of Ross Kitchen.)

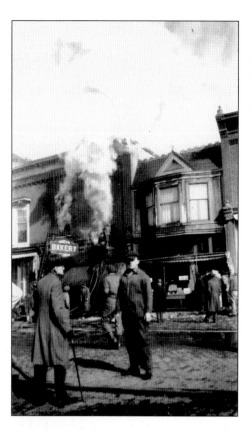

Considering the type of fire equipment available in 1924, the fire walls definitely contributed to confining the Brey Bakery fire to the bakery and the building next door. Standing with his back to the camera is John Tyler Beldin. Facing the camera is Fire Chief Bill Arlington.

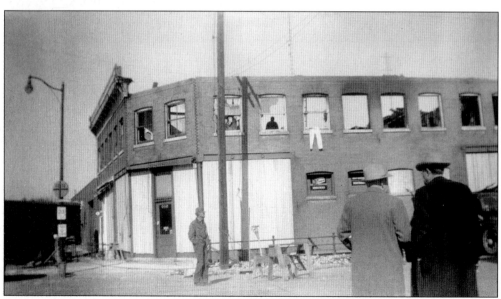

The second floor of the Majestic Hotel building suffered irreparable damage from a 1960s fire. This level had served as a hotel for many years. The first-floor portion of this historic building was salvaged and remains today as Brandt's Pharmacy. Previous businesses at street level included the Dairyman's State Bank and the Triangle Grocery. (Courtesy of Ken Holz.)

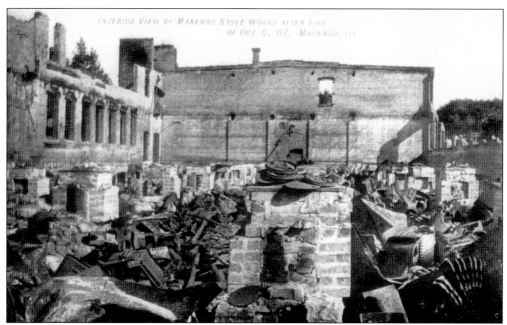

The Collins and Burgie Stove Works of Chicago was established in 1857 and incorporated in 1892 by the original founders. It was one of the oldest and best stove companies in the United States. Purchased by the Marengo Improvement Syndicate and moved to Marengo in 1892, it employed approximately 200 workers. R. M. Patrick was president, E. D. Patrick was secretary, and S. K. Bartholomew, F. W. Patrick, A. B. Coon, J. F. Warren, and A. Corson were directors. It was considered the largest stove factory west of Chicago, being responsible for many people moving to Marengo. In operation for 15 years, it burned on October 3, 1907, and was never rebuilt. The factory was located at the south end of what is now the athletic field for Zion Lutheran School. Several of their stoves are owned by local residents. (Courtesy of Michael and Barbara Bigalke.)

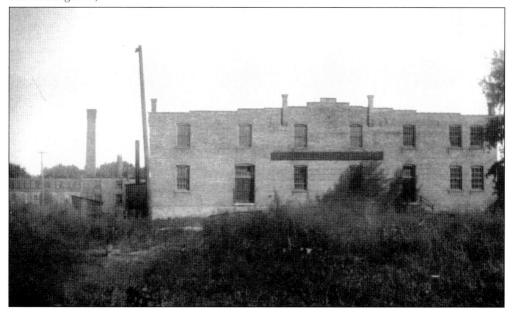

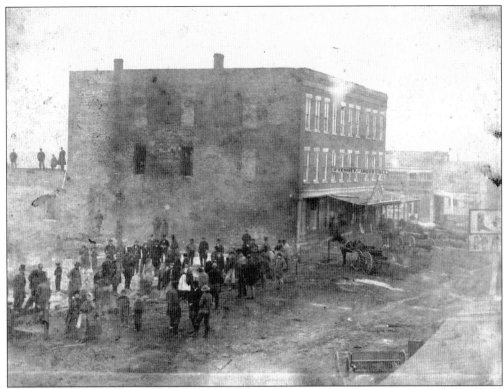

In the early 1860s, the stores just south of Lansing Block (Hall) burned. The Lansing Block building housed the McKinney and Ingersoll Mercantile business. Today it houses the offices of Dr. James Sweet, Edward Jones Investments, and others. By sheer coincidence, Dr. Sweet currently lives in the home that Eugene F. McKinney built in the late 1860s for his family on West Prairie Street. (Courtesy of McHenry County Historical Society.)

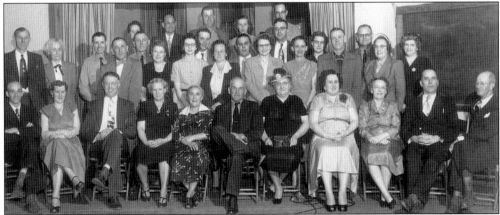

The firemen established a tradition of honoring their wives at a formal meal. In this 1940s picture, they met at the Methodist church. Space limits full identification except for the first row, from left to right are Alex and Dorothy Urqhart, Norm Piskie, Gail Benton, Emma Hauschildt, William and Bertha Piskie Sr., Gladys Kays, Elizabeth Miller, Vernon Kays, and Bill Miller. (Courtesy of Ross Kitchen.)

Henry "Hick" Nulle received the following appointments: special police officer, August 1, 1922, and city marshal (chief), September 5, 1922, through May 16, 1934. At that time, he was elected McHenry County sheriff for the first time. He was again elected sheriff to two separate terms, one in 1942 and the other in 1950. The Nulle family lived at 423 West Grant Highway. (Courtesy of Alice Nulle.)

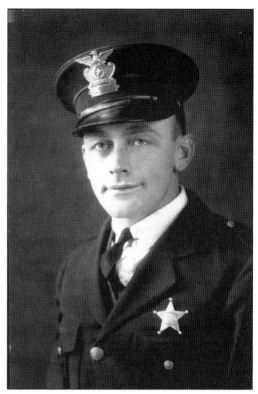

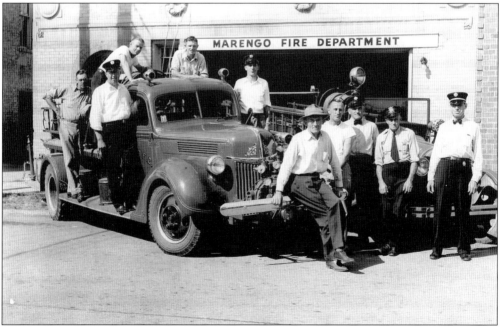

Keeping the equipment always ready to respond was the job of these firemen in the 1940s. Standing by the 1940 Darley and 1930 Ford are Bob Loomis, Norm Piskie, Whitey Willis, Clarence Zerbel, Pete Norman, Robert Morris, Clifford Kitchen, William Piskie Sr., Harold Hyde, and John Benton. (Courtesy of Ross Kitchen.)

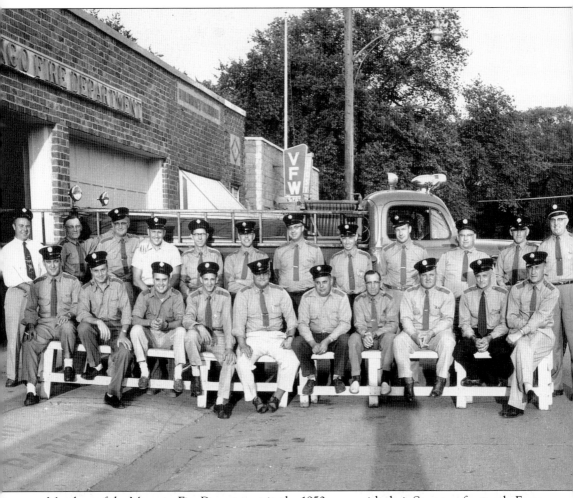

Members of the Marengo Fire Department in the 1950s pose with their Seagrave fire truck. From left to right are (first row) Bill Dusenberry, Herb Swanlund, John Dusenberry, Alex Urqhart, William Piskie Jr., Cliff Polnow, Ray Stock, Burdette Roth, Harold Hyde, and Clifford Kitchen; (second row) Glenn Crawford, George Hauschildt, Earl Ham, Duwane Johnson, Clarence Zerbel, Warren Lindsay, Erhart Kolberg, John Benton, Harold Kolberg, Lowell Brooks, William Piskie Sr., and Chief Norm Piskie. (Courtesy of Ross Kitchen.)

The old brick building at the rear of the Shurtleff Lumber and Grain on Taylor Street burned in the 1960s. This brick addition was built about 1911, when the Shurtleffs purchased the property. It held a feed grinding mill. The original buildings on the property were built in 1861 and housed the Marengo Flouring Mill. (Courtesy of Ross Kitchen.)

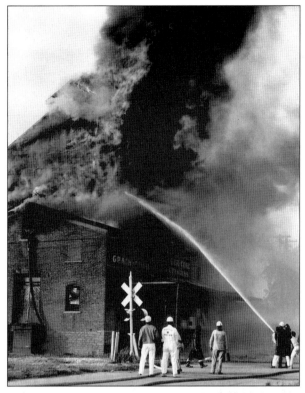

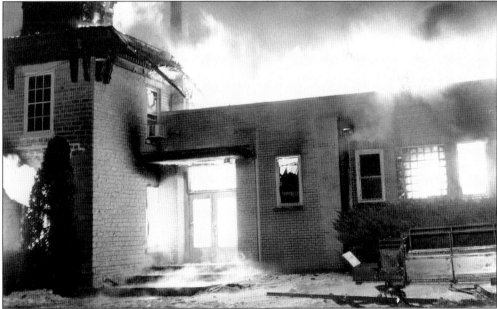

The popular Cloven Hoof Restaurant, located at 21906 West Grant Highway, was destroyed by fire on January 25, 1976. The firemen arrived at 4:30 a.m. to flames shooting over 40 feet in the air. Al and Millie Chewning owned the restaurant, which formerly was the home of the George Colver family. The home was one of the early locations of the post office. (Courtesy of Ross Kitchen.)

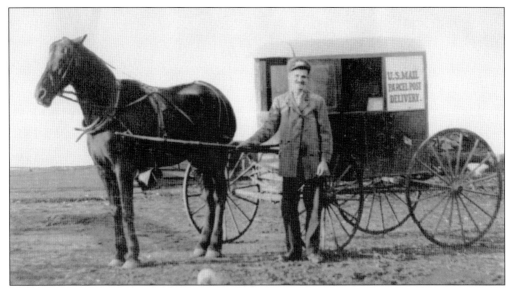

This photograph, from 1913, shows rural postal carrier Lee Grover with his last horse, Polly. Grover started carrying mail on Rural Route No. 3 in 1903. He traveled about 25 miles to serve approximately 100 families. He started out about 8:30 a.m., and was expected back by 3:30 p.m. Until about 1925, Grover still used horses in bad weather. He retired in 1953 after 50 years on the route. (Courtesy of McHenry County Historical Society.)

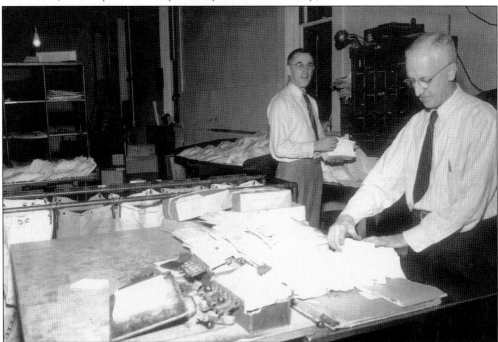

In the 1940s, the Marengo Post Office was located at 110 East Washington Street, just west of the Strahorn Memorial Library. Clair Carney was the postmaster. Shown sorting mail are Clifford Kitchen (left) and Ralph Beldin. When Christmas mail was heavy, the employees' wives helped out in the office. At that time, there were two rural carriers, two city carriers, and several clerks. (Courtesy of Shirley Kitchen.)

Eight

MARENGO'S NOTABLE RESIDENTS

Marengo native Carl Leonard Lundgren was born in 1880, graduating from Marengo High School in 1898. His services on the baseball field were always in demand. He continued playing baseball while pursuing a degree in civil engineering at the University of Illinois at Champaign. Frank Chance recruited Lundgren immediately after graduation, and he pitched for the Cubs from 1902 to 1909. During that time, the Cubs won the 1906 National League pennant and back-to-back World Series championships in 1907 and 1908. Lundgren created a second successful career in coaching, with impressive records at Princeton University, University of Michigan at Ann Arbor, and University of Illinois. Lundgren died of a heart attack on August 21, 1934. (Courtesy of Lundgren family.)

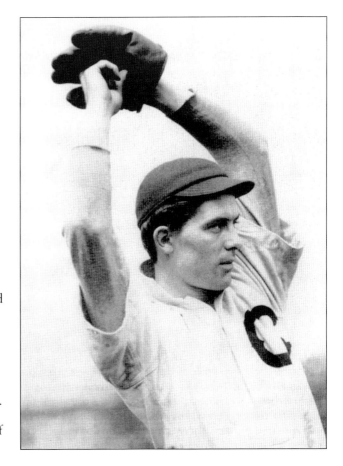

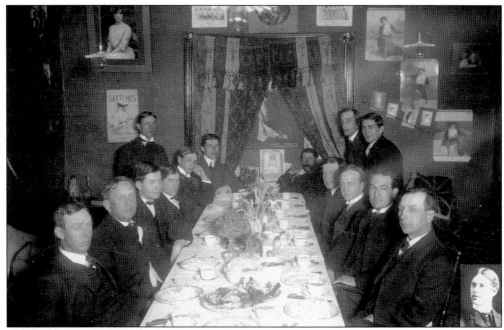

In the late 1890s, Marengo's young men organized a Stoller's Club for discussion of current topics. Identified in this group, seen here seated, clockwise from bottom left, are Ralph "Deke" Metcalf, Gabe Sampter, Daniel Boyle, Carl Lundgren, Floyd Jobe, Harley Lanning, two unidentified, S. C. "Pen" Wernham, Phil "Pub" Otis, and Judge E. D. Shurtleff. Egbert VanAlstyne is shown in the inset. (Courtesy of Dan Wernham.)

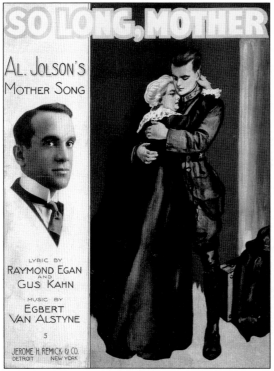

"So Long Mother," "Memories," and "In the Shade of the Old Apple Tree" are only a few of local composer Egbert VanAlstyne's 400-some music compositions. Working with many well-known lyricists such as Gus Kahn, Raymond Egan, and Harry Williams, VanAlstyne composed songs ranging from love songs to ragtime. (Courtesy of Tracy Doyle.)

Emma Rogers VanAlstyne Lanning was born to Anson and Rebecca Hart Rogers in 1856 at what is currently, 19809 East Grant Highway. At the age of 65, she pursued a four-year degree in drama and poetry at the Chicago Musical College. This prepared her for a long association with the radio station WLS. "Aunt Em," as she was known, was the mother of celebrated composer Egbert VanAlstyne.

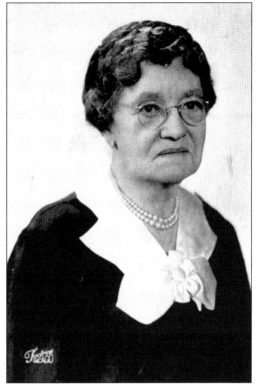

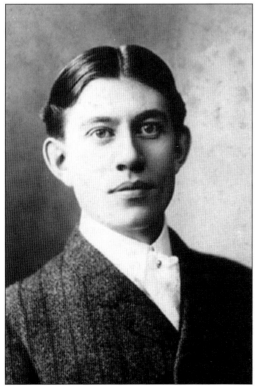

As a seven-year-old childhood musical prodigy, Egbert was playing the organ for Sunday school at the Methodist church. Egbert studied under Carolyn Coon, the classically trained daughter-in-law of Amos B. Coon, an early Marengo settler. In 1950, Egbert was honored at the Chicago Music Festival, where an apple tree had been planted in honor of his hometown and of one of his most popular songs, "In the Shade of the Old Apple Tree." It has been said that most of his big hits were not brilliant from a musical standpoint, but were tunes that touched the hearts of the listeners. "In the Shade of the Old Apple Tree" has sold over 26 million copies. "Bert" was perhaps the most diversified composer of his time. He wrote piano rags, marches, waltzes, intermezzos, comic songs, fox trots, while adding a few operettas. He died in Chicago in 1951. (Courtesy of Tracy Doyle.)

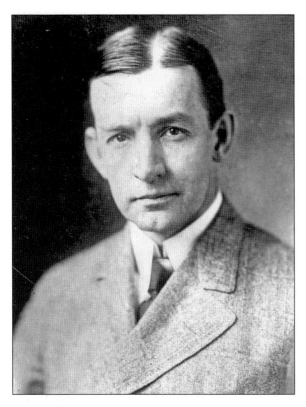

Marengo had the distinct honor of being home to the son of Vice Pres. Charles G. Dawes. Dawes was elected, along with Calvin Coolidge (pictured below, left), in 1924. At his inauguration, Dawes made a fiery, half-hour address denouncing the rules of the Senate, the seniority system, and many other actions that the senators had taken. Following his vice presidency, Dawes became the United States ambassador to the United Kingdom. His son Dana Dawes and family, wife Suzie and two sons, lived at 424 West Washington Street, for over 20 years. Dana was very involved with the Boy Scouts and other community groups. His oldest son, Charles, graduated from Marengo Community High School in 1954.

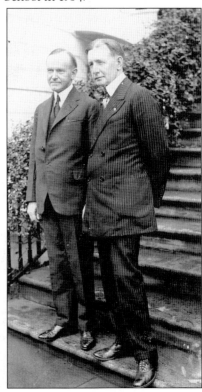

Arriving in Marengo in 1933, Ray Walters became a local celebrity as a comic postcard cartoonist, which actively lasted through 1946. Prior to his arrival in Marengo, Walters was an editorial newspaper artist. His postcards were extremely popular, containing a wealth of detail, were expertly drawn, with bright colors and often contained slice-of-life moments that many found appealing. Perhaps for his own amusement, or that of his neighbors on North State Street, he often discreetly inserted references to the local community. Notice his detour signs. All Walters would have to do today, would be to add an I-90 to his sign, and he would be right up to date! It was in 1935 that he drew the realistic picture of Marengo's settler Calvin Spencer, as well as other realistic depictions of local interest. (Courtesy of Courtney and Stephen Mack, "Walters' World.")

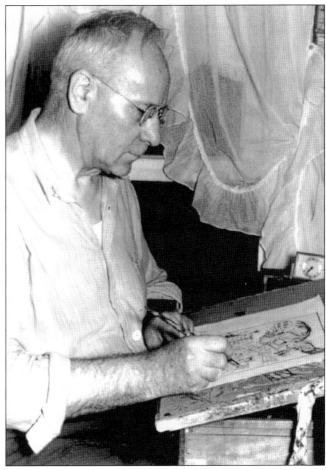

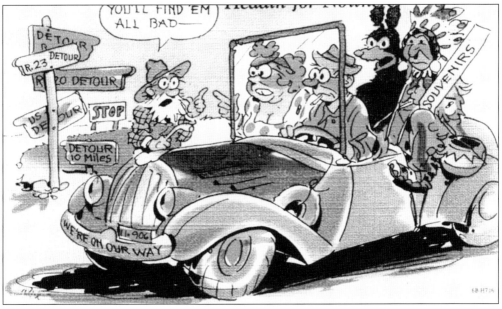

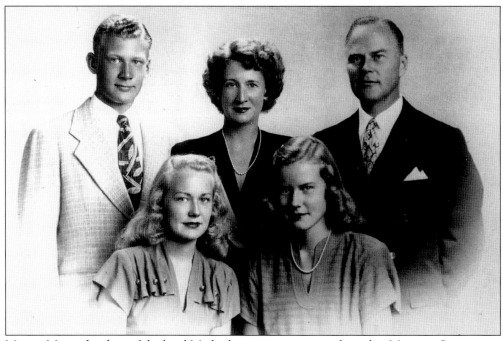

Marion Moon, daughter of the local Methodist pastor, was a popular girl in Marengo Community High School, graduating in 1921. Who would have guessed that she would become the mother of the second person to walk on the moon, Eugene "Buzz" Aldrin! Born in 1930, Buzz graduated from West Point and then joined the United States Air Force. Marion remained lifelong friends with Hazel Hyde Kitchen, often visiting her in Marengo. (Courtesy of Shirley Pinnow Kitchen.)

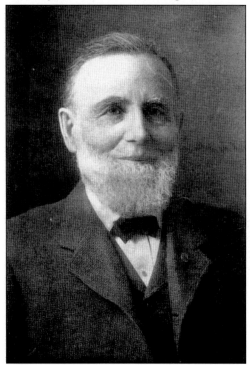

Dr. Charles C. Miller arrived in Marengo in 1856. He came equipped with medical and teaching degrees, but it was his study of honey bees that brought him to the attention of the world. Miller wrote extensively, contributing articles to *Gleanings in Bee Culture, Country Gentleman,* and *Youth's Companion.* Among the many books he authored are *A Book by P. Benson, A Year Among Bees, Forty Years Among the Bees,* and *Fifty Years Among the Bees.* His writings were translated into French, German, Swiss, Italian, Russian, and Japanese. He was referred to as the "Sage of Marengo."

Nine

MARENGO AT ARMS

Lucius W. Barber was born May 10, 1839, in Java, New York. His family moved to Riley Township in 1851. As a young man of 22, he answered the call to arms in 1861. His unit was Company D, 15th Illinois Volunteer Infantry. On October 4, 1864, he and 400 other Union soldiers were captured in a battle near Ackworth, Georgia, and incarcerated in the Andersonville, Georgia, prisoner-of-war camp. The consumption (tuberculosis) he caught there eventually killed him at the age of 32 in 1872. His memoirs were later published in book form as *The Army Memoirs of Lucius W. Barber*. In his memoirs, he says this about Ulysses S. Grant when Grant ignored orders and rushed to attack Vicksburg; "It was a perilous move, a move few military men would have dared undertake, but Grant was of that bold, sanguine nature, ever confident of success."

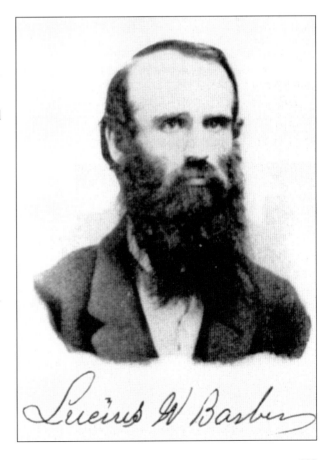

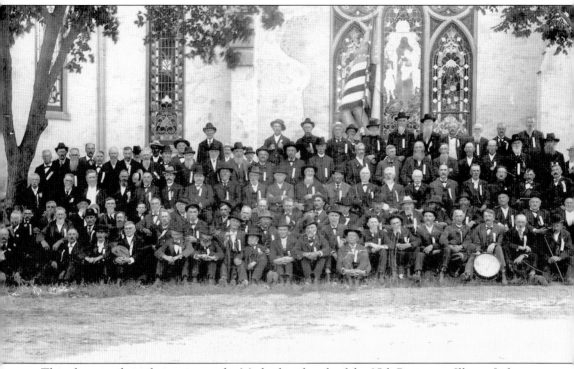

This photograph is of a reunion at the Methodist church of the 95th Regiment, Illinois Infantry Volunteers. On September 5, 1903, this same group met for their 38th annual reunion in the GAR hall in Belvidere. At the Belvidere reunion, members living in Marengo and attending included Alonzo Andrews, W. Z. Casely, John Kennedy, George Thomas, W. C. Sullivan, J. Cavner, Sam Rowland, E. O. Knapp, N. F. Colver, James Benjamin, H. M. Filmore, Andrew Sears, W. H. Sanders, Ira Webber, J. B. Babcock, Thomas Gilkerson, E. J. Goodrich, M. C. Stoddard, J. O. Adams, George Blatchford, Ahira Thompson, E. R. Morris, B. T. Henry, Jacob Grooman, John Wallace, and J. Q. Adams.

Charles W. Fillmore and his two brothers were blacksmiths in Coral, manufacturing the first plows in northern Illinois. In 1851, Charles W. married Henrietta Poole, to whom was born, John Hudson Fillmore (pictured here). John had the distinction of graduating from the United States Naval Academy at Annapolis in 1875, at the age of 17, graduating at the head of his class. He was taken ill and died in 1893 at the age of 36. His funeral was held in Marengo. (Courtesy of Dan Wernham.)

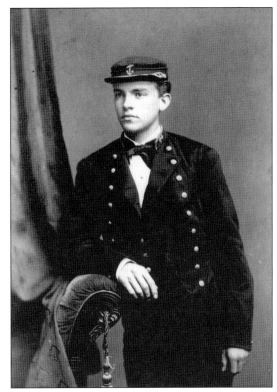

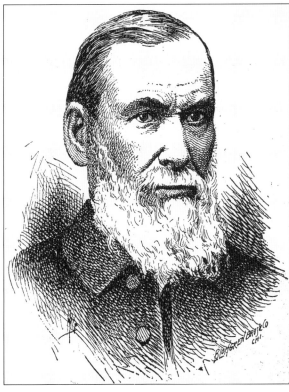

Commissioned as surgeon of the 95th Regiment, Illinois Infantry Volunteers in April 1862, Dr. John W. Green was mustered in May 6, 1863. He served two years and four months, the greater part of the time having charge of the brigade. In February 1865, he was detailed to take charge of the Third Division Field Hospital, 16th Army Corps. It was credibly reported that he was the first physician west of New York City to administer chloroform in a surgical operation. He died unexpectedly in 1893, having served the Marengo community for 46 years.

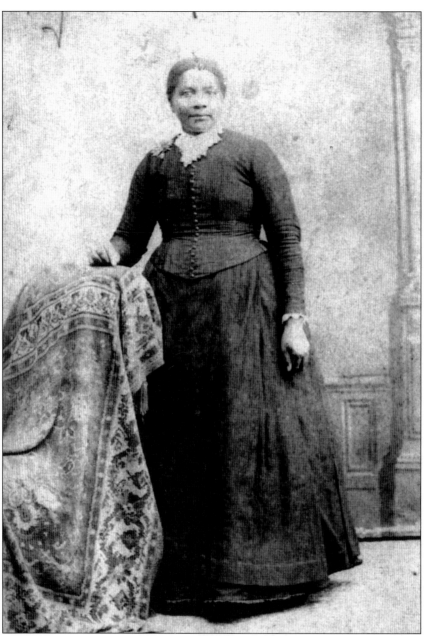

"Aunt" Rachel Harris was born a slave in Holly Springs, Mississippi, in 1838. She was attached to the 127th Illinois Infantry as an army nurse under Col. Frank Curtiss of Marengo. Her efficiency and kindheartedness became her trademark. She is credited with saving the life of Frank Curtiss's brother, Ira Curtiss. Also, on several occasions, Harris was sent through rebel lines, carrying important dispatches concealed in her hair. In 1863, Harris was sent to Marengo by Frank and Ira Curtiss to care for their ailing mother. In Marengo, she nursed many people, winning the admiration and affection of those who knew her. She was especially a favorite of the children who heard her stories about her own younger days. She passed away May 7, 1907. Her many friends attended her funeral. She is buried in the Marengo cemetery beside her husband, Josephus, and daughter, Annie.

Harold Hyde grew up in Marengo. After serving in "the big war," he engaged in the dray business, making deliveries from the railroad freight yard. He hauled coal and general merchandise as well as post office mail. Hyde was one of the dedicated keepers of Marengo's weather records, a long tradition initiated in 1855 by Orson P. Rogers. (Courtesy of Shirley Pinnow Kitchen.)

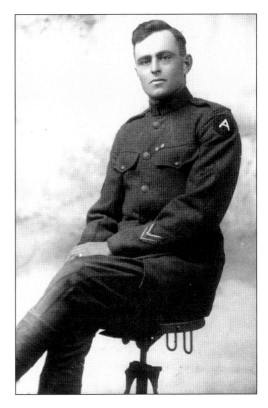

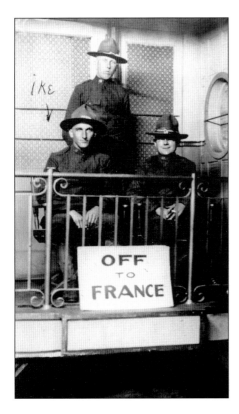

In this photograph, William "Ike" Dunker, sitting on the left, is on his way to serve in World War I. (Courtesy of Shirley Pinnow Kitchen.)

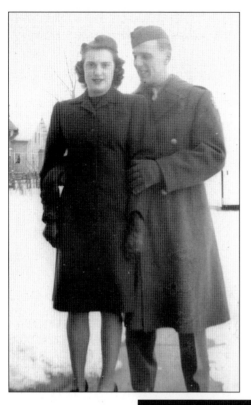

The love that U.S. Army enlistee John Brown has for his fiancée, Marcella Polnow, can be felt. Brown's squadron was part of the 50th Fighter Group. Sergeant Brown and Marcella were married November 17, 1945. He ran his own local Standard Oil delivery service and later worked many years at Arnold Engineering. Marcella was a personal secretary to Fred Kelley for many years at the Marengo Savings and Loan, presently the Chase bank. (Courtesy of Bryson Brown Carlson.)

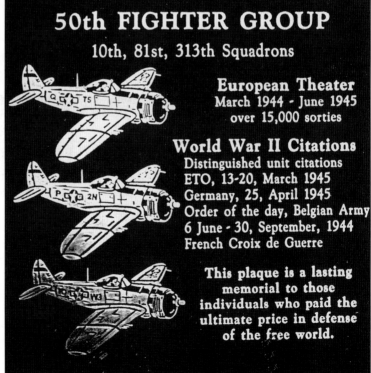

Pictured is Bob Mallory, who married Violet Anderson of Riley Township. He served with the U.S. Army in Germany during World War II. He was a longtime employee of the U.S. Postal Service. (Courtesy of Shirley Pinnow Kitchen.)

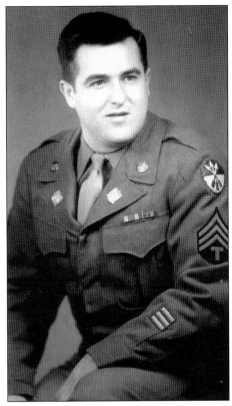

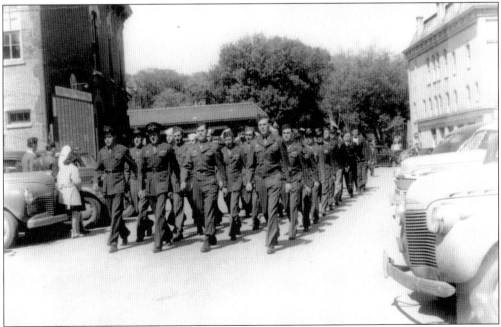

This is a very special picture in the hearts of many. The survivors proudly march by, in-step to the adulation of their hometown residents. The editors believe that Dr. Emerson C. Kunde is second from the left, front row. (Courtesy of Dan Wernham.)

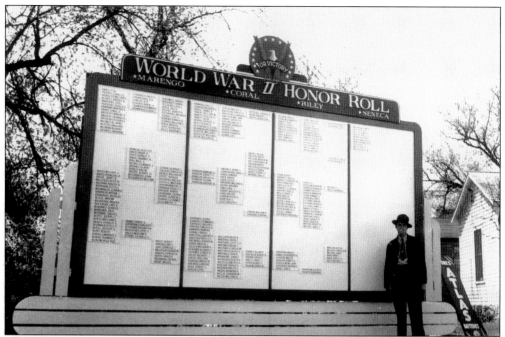

In the 1940s, the high school had a building trades class that, under the direction of their teacher Kenneth Walthers (pictured), built this honor roll with the names of all Marengo area men and women who served in World War II. The honor roll was initially erected at the intersection of Routes 20 and 23 and was later moved to the Washington Street side of 200 South State Street. (Courtesy of Marilyn Walthers Stone.)

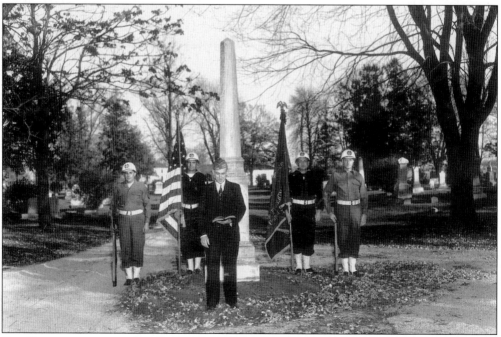

Standing at attention at the monument to the unknown soldier are the military honor guards. Their identities are unknown. (Courtesy of Michael and Barbara Bigalke)

Ten

MARENGO AT PLAY

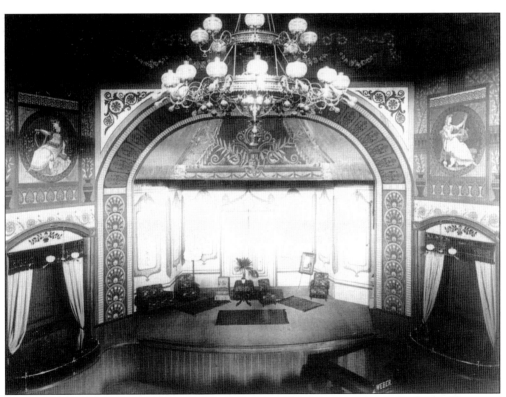

The opera house officially opened in April 1883. The first opera presented was *Chimes of Normandy* by Egbert VanAlstyne. It had a seating capacity of 750–1,000 people. Tickets cost $2. In December 1896, the audience was truly honored when VanAlstyne came home to accompany the comic opera *Rosita* with an all-home-talent cast under the direction of his former teacher Carolyn Coon. There were 15 full sets of scenery for its 25-by-50-foot stage. The beautiful frescoed ceiling and gilded walls were illuminated by over 100 gas jets. (Courtesy of McHenry County Historical Society.)

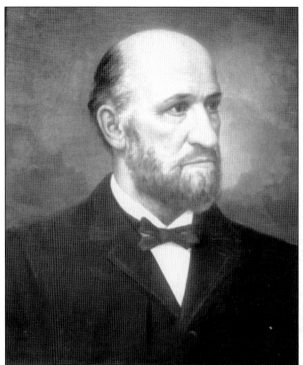

Upon the death of Richard Montgomery Patrick in 1915, the Commercial Club issued a resolution, which read in part "Whereas, in view of his success in life, we see the possibilities of real success in a so-called 'small town.' Therefore be it resolved that we recall with gratitude his life amongst us and his interest in us as a community." R. M. Patrick contributed more than $5,000 toward the building of the five churches in the city.

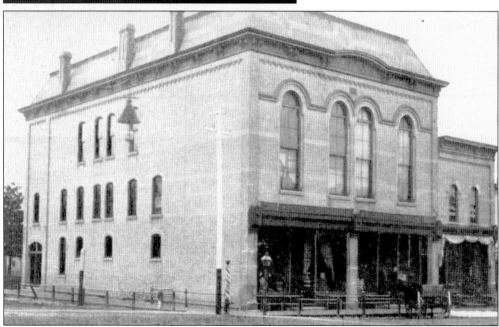

The opera house was built by Patrick at a cost of $30,000. He is quoted at saying, "The house was erected more with a view of promoting the interests of Marengo than for financial gains, and in consequence, the privilege of the use of the house is extended only to first class troupes and those known to possess nothing but the highest reputation." His death occurred at the age of 84 as a result of injuries sustained by a runaway team of horses. (Courtesy of McHenry County Historical Society.)

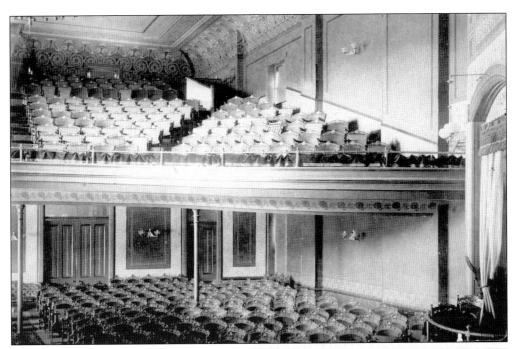

Built of Milwaukee pressed brick, the opera house was the largest building in Marengo. When built it contained only two floors. In 1916, Ernest Patrick, son of Richard Montgomery Patrick, remodeled the building, and in effect, removed the opera house area and converted it into two floors. The building was renamed the Community Building. "A floor was put in at the upper, say second floor level and a Community Club was started. Membership fees were $6. They had pool tables which you had to be a certain age to use unless you were with your parents," recalls Clifford Kitchen in *Ruminations, Reflections and Expectations*. (Courtesy of McHenry County Historical Society.)

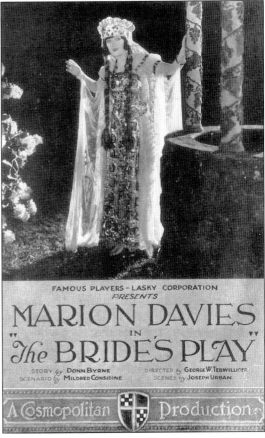

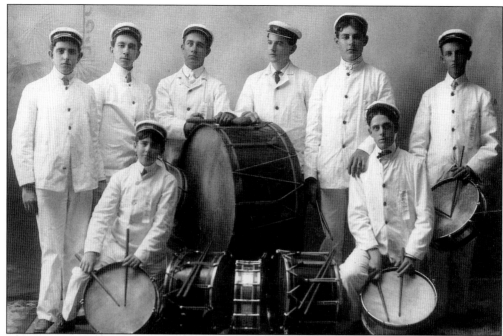

In the early 20th century, this drum corps was seen many times on the streets of Marengo. It highlighted election parades and was always a big feature at reunions and Memorial Day parades for the old 95th GAR. Pictured from left to right are (first row) Harry Patrick and Harry Eatinger; (second row) Sam Robb, Ross Cadwell, Frank Standish, George Woleben, Neal Dunham, and Ralph Beldin. This information was taken from "Rudy's Ruminations," from the *Marengo Beacon-News*.

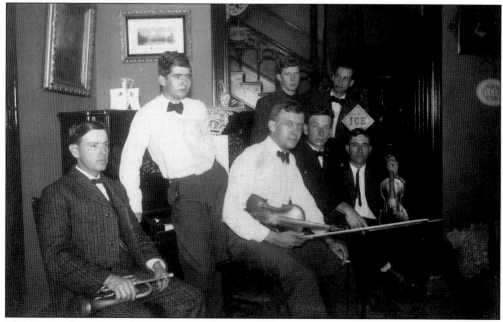

This group of young musicians met at the home of F. Wayland Patrick, 321 East Washington Street. Only the identity of Harry Patrick, second from left, is known. (Courtesy of Janice Patrick.)

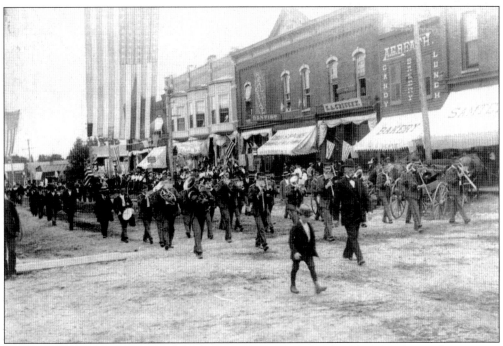

It is obvious that these old photographs are of a parade, possibly welcoming home the veterans of World War I. Ralph Beldin is one of the drummers. Also, State Street had not yet been paved. Notice the well maintained buildings, and that all of the stores had awnings. (Courtesy of Michael and Barbara Bigalke.)

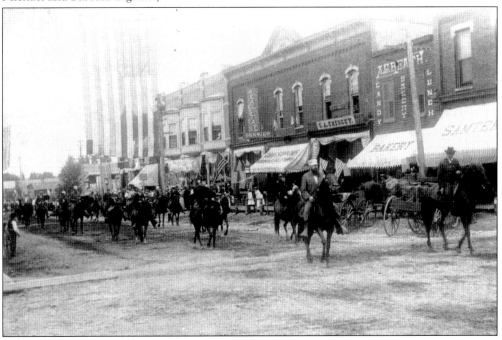

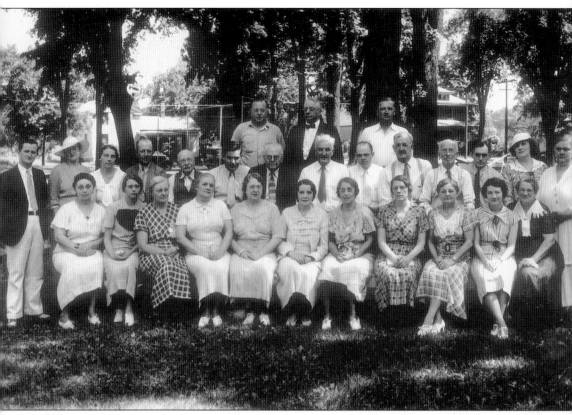

The organization and cooperation between approximately 50 residents produced an amazing celebration of Marengo's centennial in September 1935. The general chairman was Edward Dean, editor of the *Marengo Republican News*. Committee chairmen were Esther Robb; Bessie Crissey; Helen Spencer Anthony; Edna Beldin; Mary Mallory; Paul Arndt; Bess Steele; H. W. Thompson, high school music director; Artell M. Wallace; Joy Kelley; Wedell Swonguer and Charles Stokes, local businessmen; Fred Nelson, chief of police; and Rev. Edward Aikin, Methodist pastor. Literally hundreds of residents were players in the pageant, "Marengo's Romance of a Century." (Courtesy of Michael and Barbara Bigalke.)

An Old Settlers' Day program was held at Calvin Spencer Park on Sunday afternoon during the 1935 centennial celebration. It featured talks by old time and former residents, as well as former mayors, Judge Edward D. Shurtleff and Charles B. Whittemore. The Old Settlers' program had the following known participants: prayer, Rev. Edward Aikin; welcome, Mayor William Miller; comments, Judge E. D. Shurtleff; talk, C. B. Whittemore; and unveiling of monument, Maxine Ann Loomis, great-great-granddaughter of Moody Bailey. (Courtesy of Frank J. Mack family.)

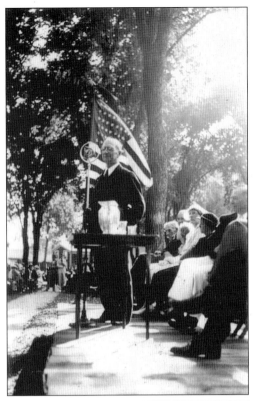

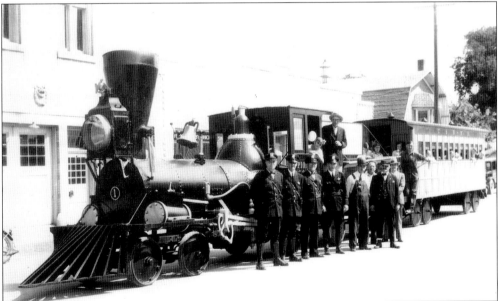

This parade replica of the *Pioneer* locomotive was in Marengo's 1935 centennial parade. The *Pioneer* rode the rails of the Galena and Chicago Union line, the first rail line built in the state. By 1851, the line extended through Marengo, making the *Pioneer* a special site to village residents and those pioneers living on farms along the rail line. (Courtesy of Michael and Barbara Bigalke.)

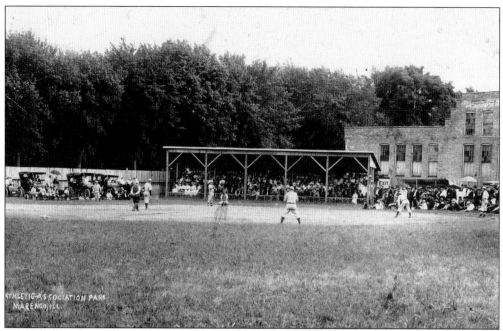

Baseball was a big source of summer fun! The Marengo ballpark, roofed bleachers and all, was home to the Marengo Athletics and Whiteys (previously called the Stars and later, Jimmy White's). The park was located on the Shurtleff flats, currently the Zion Lutheran athletic field. It was the proving ground for local baseball celebrity and popular favorite Carl Lundgren. A game played on August 28, 1908, had an attendance of 750. On a Sunday or holiday afternoon, one could hear the familiar cry, Play Ball! (Courtesy of Michael and Barbara Bigalke.)

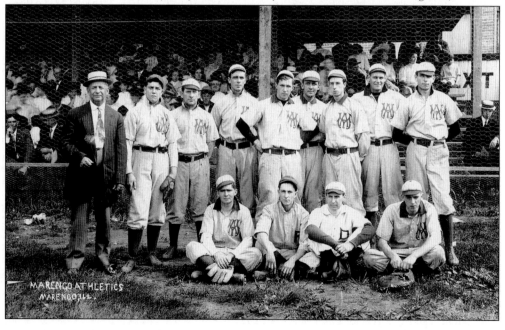

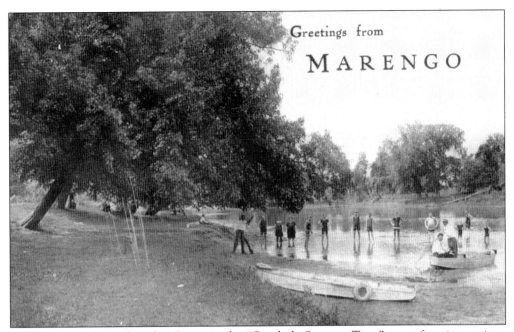

Greetings from

MARENGO

Cooling off in the Kishwaukee River, in the "Good ole Summer Time" was a favorite pastime. In the earlier times, the river was wider and deeper, holding many good memories of summer swimming and fishing. It was a favorite meeting place for young and old alike.

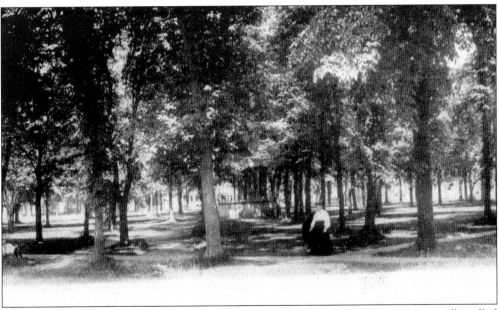

A city block in size, the land was given to the city in 1855 by Calvin Spencer. Originally called the "public square," it has for many years been known as Calvin Spencer Park. Although a city park, its supervision has been shared by others, including the American Legion, the women's club, and in recent times, by Lyn Courier. (Courtesy of Michael and Barbara Bigalke.)

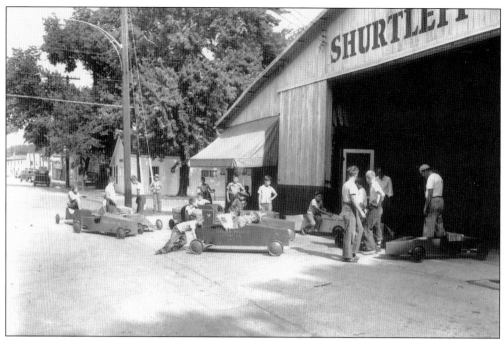

This photograph is a jewel! It shows the soapbox derby participants checking in for the upcoming race. East Prairie Street has certainly seen some big changes in this area. In this 1940s picture, Shurtleffs Lumber Company was at the height of its prosperity. (Courtesy of Frank J. Mack family.)

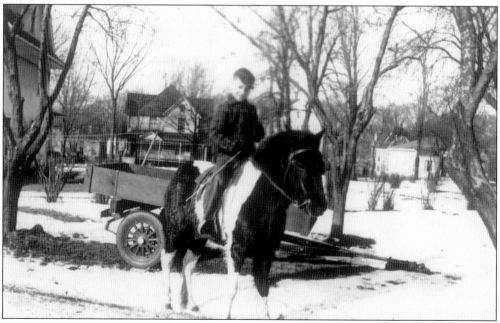

Henry Nulle went to Woodstock to see his aunt and came home to discover that Santa had come early. What a neat present! Every young child hoped for a pony to ride. At later dates in Henry's life, he was elected sheriff of McHenry County. The Nulle family lived at 423 West Grant Highway. (Courtesy of Alice Nulle.)

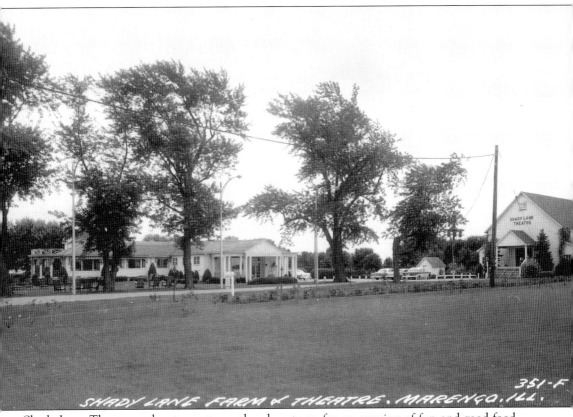

SHADY LANE FARM & THEATRE · MARENGO · ILL ·

351-F

Shady Lane Theatre and restaurant was the place to go for an evening of fun and good food. Started by Frank and Dorothy Brian in the 1940s, Shady Lane became Midwest America's top professional straw-hat theater and home of the wonderful farm-style fried chicken. Matinees were especially popular during the summertime, with tour buses regularly coming through Marengo from Chicago and the suburbs. Shady Lane provided the start for some well-known actors. (Courtesy of Michael and Barbara Bigalke.)

ACROSS AMERICA, PEOPLE ARE DISCOVERING SOMETHING WONDERFUL. THEIR HERITAGE.

Arcadia Publishing is the leading local history publisher in the United States. With more than 3,000 titles in print and hundreds of new titles released every year, Arcadia has extensive specialized experience chronicling the history of communities and celebrating America's hidden stories, bringing to life the people, places, and events from the past. To discover the history of other communities across the nation, please visit:

www.arcadiapublishing.com

Customized search tools allow you to find regional history books about the town where you grew up, the cities where your friends and family live, the town where your parents met, or even that retirement spot you've been dreaming about.

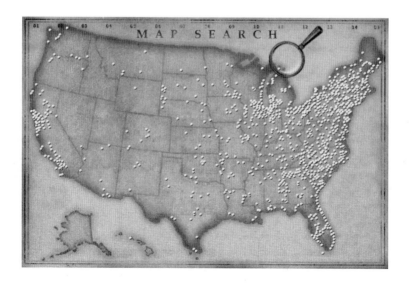